TRACING YOUR EDINBURGH ANCESTORS

FAMILY HISTORY FROM PEN & SWORD

TRACING YOUR EDINBURGH ANCESTORS

A Guide for Family Historians

Alan Stewart

Pen & Sword
FAMILY HISTORY

First published in Great Britain in 2015
PEN & SWORD FAMILY HISTORY
an imprint of
Pen & Sword Books Ltd
47 Church Street,
Barnsley
South Yorkshire,
S70 2AS

ISBN 978 1 47382 857 5

A CIP catalogue record for this book is
available from the British Library.

Typeset in Palatino and Optima by CHIC GRAPHICS

Printed and bound in England by
CPI Group (UK), Croydon, CR0 4YY

Pen & Sword Books Ltd incorporates the imprints of Pen & Sword
Archaeology, Atlas, Aviation, Battleground, Discovery, Family History,
History, Maritime, Military, Naval, Politics, Railways, Select, Social History,
Transport, True Crime, Claymore Press, Frontline Books, Leo Cooper,
Praetorian Press, Remember When, Seaforth Publishing and Wharncliffe.

For a complete list of Pen & Sword titles please contact

47 Church Street, Barnsley, South Yorkshire, S70 2AS, England
E-mail: enquiries@pen-and-sword.co.uk
Website: www.pen-and-sword.co.uk

CONTENTS

Contents

ACKNOWLEDGEMENTS

I am grateful to Rupert Harding for giving me the opportunity to write a book about my home town, and to Jen Newby for helping me with stylistic improvements.

I also express my gratitude to the Registrar General for Scotland for his kind permission to use images of statutory birth, marriage and death records; parish register baptism, marriage and burial records; and a census return.

National Records of Scotland kindly allowed me to use images of crown copyright records, including a valuation roll, testament dative, inventory, female servant tax record and window tax record.

My thanks are also due to the Statistical Accounts Online Service of the Universities of Glasgow and Edinburgh for permission to use the Midlothian parish map.

For the use of photographs available through Wikimedia under Creative Commons Attribution-Share Alike 3.0 Unported licences, I thank Kim Traynor and Martyn Gorman.

INTRODUCTION

A brief history of Edinburgh

Edinburgh has been the capital of Scotland for about 600 years. Following the murder of King James I of Scotland in Perth on 20 February 1437, the Scottish court moved to Edinburgh Castle, which was considered to be much safer than the royal palace in Dunfermline, the previous capital. It was not until 1532, however, that Edinburgh officially became the Scottish capital.

Known as the 'Athens of the North', the city is the centre of Scottish banking, medicine, architecture, law and publishing, and the home of Scotland's National Gallery, National Library and National Museum. Edinburgh is also the location of the Queen's official residence in Scotland, meeting-place of the General Assembly of the Church of Scotland, home of the internationally-renowned Edinburgh Festival and Royal Military Tattoo and, since 1999, the seat of the devolved Scottish Government.

Edinburgh Castle is situated on a lava plug from a long-extinct volcano. The area now called the 'Old Town' grew up on the highest point of the castle rock's long tail, which was created by earth being pushed round behind the rock during the last glacial period.

Edinburgh has grown in size considerably over the years, and the present City of Edinburgh unitary authority includes the formerly separate burghs of Canongate, Calton and Portsburgh (added to the city in 1856), Portobello (1896), Leith (1920) and Queensferry (1975).

The city also covers the former parish of St Cuthbert's, where the building of the 'New Town' began in 1767; the parishes of Cramond, Corstorphine, Colinton, Liberton and Duddingston, which became part of Edinburgh in 1920; as well as the parishes of Dalmeny, Kirkliston, Ratho and Currie (to the west and south-west of Edinburgh), which were added as a result of the local government reorganisation of 1975.

Musselburgh, immediately to the east of Edinburgh, has never been under the city's authority. Formerly a burgh within Midlothian, Musselburgh became part of the East Lothian district of the new

Lothian region in 1975. Following the further local government re-organisation into unitary authorities in 1996, Musselburgh remains in East Lothian.

The first part of this book tells the story of Edinburgh and its surrounding towns and villages from around 8500 BC up to the present day, featuring many colourful characters involved in the history of 'Auld Reekie' and its Old and New Towns.

Edinburgh genealogy

There's a joke in genealogy circles about people who stop their car outside the local archives, so they can just pop in and pick up their family tree. It's a joke because – unless you belong to royalty, the aristocracy or the 'gentry' (untitled landowners) – you have to compile your family tree yourself.

With Scottish ancestry, however, many of the records you need to consult have been digitised and made available online. These include: birth, marriage and death certificates (from 1855 onwards); census returns (from 1841-1911); Church of Scotland baptism, marriage and burial records (from 1553 at the earliest up to 1854); Roman Catholic baptism, marriage and burial records (from the early eighteenth century); wills and inventories (from 1513 onwards); and records of the British armed forces.

The many genealogical records relating to Edinburgh are described in detail within the second part of this book; both those that are accessible online and others that may require a trip to what Robert Louis Stevenson called 'the ancient and famous metropolis of the North'.

In addition, several appendices cover genealogy websites, relevant family history societies, and Edinburgh's many archives, museums, art galleries, castles and palaces.

The Scottish naming pattern

A 'naming pattern' was formerly used among Scottish families, whereby the first son was named after his paternal grandfather, the second son after his maternal grandfather, and the third son after his father. In the same way, the first daughter would be called after her maternal grandmother, the second daughter after her paternal grandmother and the third daughter after her mother.

It can be helpful to be aware of this naming pattern when conducting genealogical research, although it wasn't followed religiously, especially in cases of illegitimacy. The pattern tends not to be used nowadays, as children are given forenames according to their parents' preference, rather than those that have been passed down the family. (I should have been called Ralph, after my paternal grandfather, Ralph Craig Stewart, but my mother didn't like the name Ralph. My grandfather was named after his mother's father, Ralph Craig, who was in turn named after Ralph Haliburton, his maternal grandfather.)

In the past, some forenames could be used interchangeably with others (e.g. Peter and Patrick, Jean and Janet, Donald and Daniel), and there are also Gaelic versions of some English-language names, such as Alistair and Alexander, Iain and John, Hamish and James.

Patronymics

In a patronymic naming system (such as the system still in use today in Iceland), a man or woman will use the name of their father, plus 'son' or 'daughter', instead of a fixed surname. For example, I would be 'Alan Williamson', as my father's forename was William. He, however, would have been 'William Ralphson', as his father's forename was Ralph.

Patronymics survived in the Scottish Highlands and Islands into the eighteenth century (and even into the nineteenth century in Shetland). After that, the patronymic was replaced by a fixed patronymic-style surname, such as MacDonald or MacLeod.

Surnames in Edinburgh and Midlothian

According to the General Register Office for Scotland (now combined with the National Archives of Scotland – formerly the Scottish Record Office – as the National Records of Scotland), the most common surnames in Edinburgh around the years 1999-2001 were:

Smith	Thomson
Robertson	Scott
Anderson	Stewart
Brown	Campbell
Wilson	Young

A century earlier, the list of the most common surnames in Midlothian was almost identical:

Brown	Anderson
Smith	Scott
Robertson	Stewart
Wilson	Campbell
Thomson	Henderson

You can read an Occasional Paper by Neil Bowie and GWL Jackson on 'Surnames in Scotland over the past 140 years' at http://tinyurl.com/pgqbjve.

Scottish counties and parishes

Before the first major reorganisation of Scottish local government in 1975 (a year later than in England and Wales), the Lothians area consisted of three counties: West Lothian (known as Linlithgowshire until 1924), Midlothian (Edinburghshire until 1890) and East Lothian (Haddingtonshire until 1921). In 1900, Edinburgh became one of four 'counties of cities' in Scotland (the other three were Glasgow, Aberdeen and Dundee).

In 1891, parish and county boundaries were altered so that most parishes lay within one county only, and did not extend over the county boundary into a second, or even a third, county. The parish of Cramond, for instance, had previously been located mainly on the east bank of the River Almond in Midlothian, but was also partly on the west bank of the river in West Lothian. In 1891, the western part was transferred to the parish of Dalmeny and a small part of Dalmeny (Turnhouse Farm) transferred to Cramond.

Kirkliston, on the other hand, had been situated mainly in West Lothian, but with two small parts of the parish in Midlothian. One of those two sections, a detached area (around Listonshiels) to the south of Currie in Midlothian, was transferred to that parish. The Government-appointed Boundary Commissioners had originally intended to transfer the other area (which lay on the eastern bank of the River Almond) to the parish of Ratho in Midlothian, but in fact, no change was made.

Chapter 1

EDINBURGH BEFORE SCOTLAND

1.1 The Edinburgh volcano

Edinburgh has been called the 'Athens of the North' due to its construction on seven hills. These distinctive hills were created by volcanic activity way, way back in the far distant past. Around 350,000,000 years ago, a volcano erupted where the Castle Rock is today, followed by at least a dozen eruptions in what is now Holyrood Park.

After each eruption, the volcano's many vents filled with blocks of lava and volcanic ash, known as agglomerate. Once the volcano had become totally extinct, the land subsided and the volcano ended up under the sea, below a thick layer of sediment. Several million years later, the sedimentary and volcanic layers were raised by the movement of the continents, and mountains were formed. These peaks were then worn away by gradual erosion, leaving behind the rocky hills visible today, the largest of which are Arthur's Seat, the Salisbury Crags, the Whinny Hill, Calton Hill and the Castle Rock.

At roughly the same time, other volcanoes formed the East and West Craiglockhart Hills, while some 50,000,000 years previously, earlier volcanic activity had created Blackford Hill, the Braid Hills and the Pentlands.

The columns of basalt known as Samson's Ribs were formed inside the Arthur's Seat volcano from the remaining molten rock within a vent after one of the eruptions. These columns, which lie to the south of Arthur's Seat itself, are similar to those in Fingal's Cave on the island

'View of Edinburgh from Blackford Hill, 2013' by Kim Traynor. (Available under a Creative Commons Attribution-Share Alike 3.0 Unported licence at http://commons. wikimedia.org/wiki/File:View_of_Edinburgh_from_Blackford_Hill_2.jpg)

of Staffa and at the Giant's Causeway in County Antrim, Northern Ireland.

1.2 The Ice Age

We are at present living in a warm spell (an 'interglacial') in the fifth ice age, which began over 2,500,000 years ago. During the cold phases ('glacial periods'), the northern part of the island of Britain, including Edinburgh, has been covered many times by a layer of ice hundreds of metres thick. The last glacial period within the current ice age lasted from about 110,000 years ago to 12,000 years ago, when the current interglacial, the Holocene, began.

In each glacial period, ice that had built up in Scotland's Highlands and Southern Uplands merged in the Central Lowlands and flowed east across the Edinburgh area. The scouring action brought about by the ice sheet wore away the earth around the lava plug of the Castle Rock, leaving valleys to the north (the former Nor' Loch, now Princes Street

Gardens) and south (the Grassmarket) and a long earthen tail from west to east (the Royal Mile from Edinburgh Castle to Holyrood Palace).

The resulting landscape had many hollows, which filled with water and became lochs. In the Edinburgh area, several lochs have been drained during the last thousand years: the Nor' Loch, the Borough Loch (now the Meadows), Corstorphine Loch and Gogar Loch. Duddingston Loch, although reduced in size, still exists. Holyrood Park's other two lochs, St Margaret's and Dunsapie, were created in the mid-nineteenth century out of marshland.

1.3 Prehistoric Edinburgh

About 14,000 years ago, once the covering of ice had melted away, Middle Stone Age hunter-gatherers gradually made their way north to what we now call Scotland. In the Edinburgh area, a settlement at Cramond has been dated to about 8500 BC. Much later traces have also been found of people living on the Castle Rock (about 850 BC, during the late Bronze Age), where evidence has been uncovered of a settlement of round houses. In addition, some of the cultivation terraces visible on the hillsides of Holyrood Park may date back to Bronze Age and certainly Iron Age times.

Holyrood Park contains a number of defensive ramparts, prehistoric houses and cultivation terraces. These have probably survived because the park's hills, although relatively low-lying (Arthur's Seat is 251 metres above sea level, while Crow Hill and the Nether Hill are about 237 metres, and Whinny Hill and the Salisbury Crags about 175 metres), seem like a range of small mountains when compared to the surrounding area and were therefore unsuitable for modern house-building.

1.4 The Romans

After the Romans invaded the south of Britain in 43 AD, they spent the next four decades either conquering the native peoples or making alliances with them. By about 80 AD, the Roman army under Julius Agricola, the Roman governor of the province of Britannia (England and Wales), had arrived in what they called Caledonia (the south of what is now Scotland), where the occupying forces built a line of forts between the Firths of Forth and Clyde.

Agricola advanced to Perth and beyond, and defeated the Britons of Caledonia in 84 AD at the Battle of Mons Graupius, the site of which is unknown. Various suggestions have been put forward for the possible location, including Bennachie in Aberdeenshire and Moncrieffe Hill in Perthshire. Agricola's son-in-law, the writer Cornelius Tacitus, names in his book Agricola the leader of the Britons as Calgacus and attributes to him a speech to his troops in which he denounces the Romans: 'You Caledonians have never been slaves … The Romans … rob, kill and rape, and this they call Roman rule. They make a desert and they call it peace.'

Despite his victory (or perhaps, as Tacitus suggests, due to the Emperor's jealousy of it), Agricola was recalled to Rome. Wars on the Continent and unrest in what is now Wales seem to be the most probable reasons why the Roman army withdrew to the south between about 86 and 90 AD.

Over 30 years later, the Emperor Hadrian arrived in Britain and ordered a wall to be built between present-day Newcastle and Carlisle. Construction of Hadrian's Wall was begun in the year 122 and continued for about six years. In 142, Hadrian's successor, the Emperor Antoninus Pius, re-occupied the land north of Hadrian's Wall and ordered a turf wall and ditch to be built connecting Agricola's line of forts. At the same time, the Romans constructed new forts at Cramond

(*Caer Amon*, 'the fort on the river Almond' in Old Welsh) and Inveresk, near Musselburgh. The Antonine Wall was completed by 154, but after a further eight years, the Roman army withdrew to Hadrian's Wall.

The Cramond fort was re-occupied by the Romans when the Emperor Septimius Severus came to Britain and re-invaded what is now the south of Scotland in 209, subsequently re-occupying the Antonine Wall. Severus became ill in 210, however, and died at Eboracum (York) in 211. Although Severus's son Caracalla tried to continue his father's campaign, the Romans soon withdrew to Hadrian's Wall once more.

Although the Romans are not known to have stationed troops on the Castle Rock itself, it seems highly unlikely that they would have ignored it, given the rock's strategic position. Many Roman artefacts have been found in the centre of Edinburgh, including busts of Severus and his empress Julia Domna, who had accompanied him on his British campaign. In 1997, a large carved stone was discovered in the mud at the mouth of the River Almond in Cramond, depicting a lioness devouring a bound male prisoner. The stone is thought to have been a Roman sculpture brought to the area for the tomb of an important commander.

1.5 Din Eidyn and Edwinesburg

During the Roman period, the people who lived in what became the Lothians, Berwickshire and Northumberland were called the Votadini, Wotadini or Otadini by the Romans. The Votadini were Britons whose language was a form of Old Welsh. In the British language, the people were known as the Guotodin, which became Gododdin in Modern Welsh (pronounced 'Godothin').

Their main centre before about 400 was the hill in modern East Lothian now known as Traprain Law (previously called Dunpendyrlaw), which had been used as a burial place for nearly 2,000 years. Remains of ramparts have been found dating back to around 1000 BC, and these were modified and rebuilt many times over the years.

In the early fifth century, the site was abandoned and Din Eidyn, meaning 'the fort on the slope', now Edinburgh, became the Gododdin's chief town. (The Gaelic version of the name, Dùn Èideann, provided the inspiration for the name of the second-largest city on New Zealand's South Island.) This was around the time when the Angles travelled across the sea from an area around the boundary between modern Germany and Denmark and arrived in the north of what is now England. Subsequently, the Angles established kingdoms in Deira (now East Yorkshire) and Bernicia (now Northumberland and County Durham.)

Bernicia had previously been part of the Gododdin lands. It seems that an attempt to recover this area prompted the march of around 300 Gododdin warriors from Din Eidyn to do battle with the Angles at Catraeth (probably now Catterick, in Yorkshire) around the year 600 (as described in an early poem in Welsh, '*Y Gododdin*' or 'The Gododdin', by the poet Aneirin).

The Gododdin, under their king, Mynyddawg Mwynfawr (Mynyddawg the Wealthy), were defeated by the Angles, and three years later, an army led by King Æthelfrith of Bernicia defeated a Scots army belonging to King Aedan of Dalriada (the modern Argyll) at an unidentified location named *Degsastan*. Æthelfrith then gained control over Deira too, and created the kingdom of Northumbria, after which the Angles advanced further into what are now the Scottish Borders and the Lothians. A record in *The Annals of Ulster* refers to Edinburgh being under siege in the year 638, and by 650 the Lothians had become part of Northumbria.

After Æthelfrith's death in 616, he was succeeded by King Edwin of the House of Deira. Edwin, who had been in exile (possibly in modern north Wales), reigned until 633. As part of Northumbria, Edinburgh was known as Edwinesburg, and it was at one time thought that the city had been founded by (or at least, named after) Edwin.

Edinburgh, the Lothians and the Scottish Borders remained in Angle (and then English) hands for more than 300 years. The Pictish Chronicle states that 'oppidum Eden' (Edinburgh) was handed over to the Scots in the reign of King Indulf (954-962). Around 973, the area between the Firth of Forth and the River Tweed was granted to Kenneth II, King of Scots, in return for his homage to King Edgar of England, great-grandson of Alfred the Great and ancestor of Robert the Bruce.

Chapter 2

THE OLD TOWN

2.1 The thirteenth century and earlier: Saint Margaret and her children

The oldest building in Edinburgh is St Margaret's Chapel in the castle (see Appendix A6.2), which was built in the early twelfth century. It was the only part of the castle to avoid demolition in 1314, under the orders of King Robert the Bruce, to avoid it falling into the hands of the English army. This ancient chapel was dedicated not to the memory of a Scottish saint, but to an Englishwoman who was born in Hungary.

Queen Margaret (as she was then) was already ill and she died in Edinburgh Castle just days after hearing of the death of her husband, Malcolm III ('Malcolm Canmore'), and her eldest son, Edward, at the Battle of Alnwick on 13 November 1093. Just over 150 years later, Margaret was canonised by Pope Innocent IV.

Three of Margaret's sons became Kings of the Scots: Edgar (who reigned from 1097-1107), Alexander I (1107-1124) and David I (1124-1153), while her daughter Edith (later known as Matilda) married Henry I of England on 11 November 1100. It was through Edith/Matilda's line, however, that later English monarchs are descended from the pre-Conquest Anglo-Saxon kings. Matilda and Henry's daughter, Matilda (also known as Maud), became the Empress of Germany and went on to fight against King Stephen for the English throne, during the civil war known as the 'Anarchy'. The present royal family are doubly descended from the Anglo-Saxon monarchs, as most Scottish monarchs from Edgar onwards are descended from the Anglo-Saxons through Queen Margaret.

In medieval and earlier times, the area to the east of Edinburgh Castle, where the esplanade now is, was much lower than it is now, with forty steps leading up to the castle entrance. It was only after the demolition of a defensive battery called the Spur, in about 1649, that a narrow raised roadway was created between Castle Hill and the castle

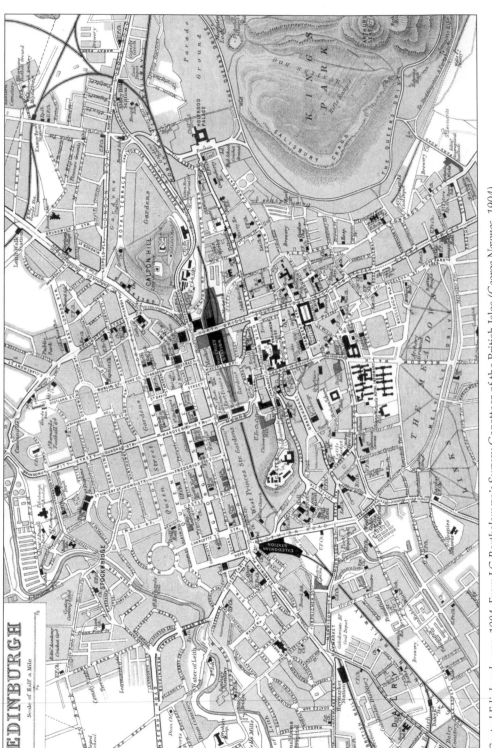

Central Edinburgh map, 1904. From J G Bartholomew's Survey Gazetteer of the British Isles (George Newnes, 1904).

itself. The level of the esplanade area was gradually raised with earth excavated from the site of the Royal Exchange in 1753.

Edinburgh grew up at the top of the slope of what later became the 'Royal Mile' from the castle to Holyrood Palace. According to the English chronicler Simeon of Durham, in 854 Edinburgh was only a large village. Yet, by the twelfth century, David I, who had spent many years at the English court, introduced the 'burgh' to Scotland as an administrative area. The first two burghs were Berwick (now in England) and Roxburgh (destroyed in the mid-fifteenth century), but by 1130 Edinburgh had become one of the King's new 'royal burghs'.

During the thirteenth and fourteenth centuries, the castle was held by the English from time to time, but by the latter part of the reign of David II in the 1360s, the Scottish parliament had met on several occasions in Edinburgh, which by then also had a mint.

2.2 The fourteenth and fifteenth centuries: the arrival of the Stewarts

After the accession of Robert II, the first Stewart king, in 1371, Edinburgh became the chief burgh in Scotland, although not the official capital. At that time, the city consisted of around 4,000 houses, the majority of which, together with St Giles' Church and Holyrood Abbey, were burned in a five-day attack by Richard II of England in 1385. Both Richard (in 1385) and his successor Henry IV (in 1400) attacked the castle, but neither force captured it.

James I was frequently in residence at Holyrood, where he received the submission of Alexander MacDonald, Lord of the Isles, in 1429. The following year, his son (the future James II) was born at Holyrood. In March 1437, James II was also crowned at Holyrood, a month after the murder of his father at Perth. This was the first time for many centuries that the coronation of a King of Scots had not taken place at Scone in Perthshire.

Edinburgh became the seat of the Court (or Parliament) of the Four Burghs in 1452, from which year it has been judged the capital of Scotland. The original four burghs were Berwick, Roxburgh, Stirling and Edinburgh, with the former two replaced by Linlithgow and Lanark in 1369.

James IV's first Parliament met in Edinburgh in 1488. At Holyrood in 1495, the King entertained Perkin Warbeck, the pretender to the

King James IV (1473-1513). From Francis Watt's Book of Edinburgh Anecdote *(T N Foulis, 1912).*

English throne who claimed to be Richard, the younger of the 'Princes in the Tower' and son of Edward IV of England.

2.3 The sixteenth century: the Battle of Flodden and Mary, Queen of Scots

Perkin Warbeck was unsuccessful in his attempt to become King of England, and James IV later married Margaret Tudor, daughter of Henry VII of England and sister of Henry VIII, with the marriage taking place at Holyrood in 1503.

Ten years later, however, Scotland was once again at war with England, and this resulted in a disastrous battle just over the border at Flodden in Northumberland, in which James IV and thousands of Scots died. The old Scots folk tune 'The Floo'ers o' the Forest' commemorates the loss of Scotland's young men (although the best-known words to the tune were written by Jean Elliot in 1756).

Queen Margaret Tudor (1489-1541). From Francis Watt's Book of Edinburgh Anecdote *(T N Foulis, 1912).*

As a result of the battle, Edinburgh gained a new surrounding wall, known as the Flodden Wall, taking in the area of the Grassmarket and the Cowgate, which had lain outside the earlier King's Wall, built by James II in 1427.

Edinburgh is a long way from the Highlands, where most clan battles were fought, but in 1520, a skirmish between a Lowland and a Border family took place in the city's High Street. Known in popular legend as 'Cleanse the Causeway', the fight was between the Hamiltons, led by the Earl of Arran, and the Douglases, under their chief the Earl of Angus. About eighty of the supporters of the Hamiltons were killed, with the Earl of Arran escaping across the Nor' Loch.

In 1534, Scotland was still a Roman Catholic country, in which Protestant martyrs Norman Gourlay and David Straiton were burnt at the stake at Greenside, by the Calton Hill. Eight years later, a further six men suffered the same fate on Castle Hill.

In July 1543, the Treaty of Greenwich was signed by Scotland and England, stipulating that the infant Mary, Queen of Scots would marry Edward, the son of Henry VIII, when she reached the age of ten.

Mary, Queen of Scots (1542-1587). From Francis Watt's Book of Edinburgh Anecdote *(T N Foulis, 1912).*

However, in December of the same year the treaty was rejected by the Scottish Parliament.

Henry VIII was not pleased and in response he began what was known as the 'Rough Wooing'. Two hundred English ships arrived in the Firth of Forth on May Day 1544, bringing soldiers under the command of the Earl of Hertford, who disembarked at Newhaven and took control of Leith. Hertford's men then broke down the gates of Edinburgh and prepared to attack the castle.

Its defenders, however, fired on the English army, killing many officers and destroying a cannon. Hertford therefore withdrew his men from the attack on the castle and retaliated by setting fire to many parts of Edinburgh. For several days, the English troops continued to burn the city and destroy places around it, in particular, Craigmillar Castle (see Appendix A6.4), where the Edinburgh merchants had stored their goods for safekeeping. Holyrood Abbey and Palace were also burnt. Further attacks followed in 1547, but in support of the Scots, King Henri II of France sent 6,000 soldiers the next year, who were garrisoned at Leith until 1560 (see Chapter 5.1).

In 1555, John Knox, the Protestant reformer, arrived in Edinburgh and stirred up the populace with his preaching. The following year, Mary of Guise, the mother of Queen Mary and Regent of Scotland, complained to the city magistrates when a reformist mob destroyed some statues in St Giles' Cathedral in accordance with Knox's stance against idolatry.

Mary, Queen of Scots married the heir to the French throne in April 1558, and became Queen of France in July the next year when her husband was crowned King François II. His reign was cut short when he died of an ear infection in December 1560, so Mary returned to Scotland the following August. (For more information about Mary, Queen of Scots, see Appendix A6.1.)

In the year 1560 the Scottish Parliament abolished Papal jurisdiction over Scotland in favour of Protestantism, as had already happened in England. The Edinburgh town council decreed that all 'idolaters, fornicators, and adulterers' should be banished from the city, that public fairs, markets, sports and games should no longer take place on a Sunday, and that no shops or taverns should be open, or goods sold, during church services.

Between 1567 and 1573, there was a civil war between the supporters of Queen Mary (the Queen's men, as they called themselves) and those of her son, the infant James VI (known as the King's men). In 1571, a Queen's Parliament sat in Edinburgh, while a King's Parliament sat in the Canongate. Two years later, the castle – then held by the Queen's men – was captured by their opponents, with the help of an English army.

2.4 The seventeenth century: the Union of the Crowns, the Covenanters and the Darien scheme

In March 1603, James VI inherited the English throne through his great-grandmother Margaret Tudor, and moved to London, where he was crowned James I of England in July of that year. James's only return visit to his birthplace was in 1618. It was a sign of the changed times for Edinburgh that when James died in March 1625, his son Charles I was crowned King of England in February 1626, but he was not formally crowned King of Scotland until he visited Edinburgh in June 1633.

Charles I attempted to impose the forms of the Church of England on to the Scottish Church in 1637. The New Statistical Account reported in 1845 that:

> 'Edinburgh was made the seat of a diocese, comprehending the three Lothians and part of Berwickshire. The church of St. Giles formed the cathedral.
>
> 'On Sunday, the 23rd of July, the English liturgy was first read in this church. Both the Archbishops, a number of the Privy Council, the Lords of Session and magistrates of the city, with a great concourse of people were assembled. All was profound silence till the Dean of Edinburgh arrayed in his surplice opened the service book. On this, one of the old women near the pulpit exclaimed, "Out, out, ye fause thief, do ye say the mass at my lug?"
>
> 'This was followed by clapping of hands, hisses, imprecations, and yellings of scorn. Lindsay, Bishop of Edinburgh, with a view to appease the tumult, ascended the pulpit, but immediately a stool was hurled at his head by Janet Geddes. The Archbishop of St Andrews, the Lord Chancellor, and others attempted but in vain to stem the torrent of popular indignation; the greater part of the multitude now left the church at the persuasion of the magistrates, and the service was hurried over amid much interruption both from within and the crowd without.'

Presbyterianism had been established as the form of Protestantism practised in Scotland by an Act of the Scottish Parliament in 1592, and a National Covenant was drawn up in 1638, pledging the maintenance of the Protestant religion and loyalty to the king. The Covenant was signed by a large number of people in Greyfriars Churchyard, and copies were sent to other towns and cities for signature. In 1640, the Covenant was accepted by the Scottish Parliament, and its supporters became known as Covenanters.

After the execution of Charles I in 1649, his son was proclaimed King of Scotland and he was crowned Charles II in Scone on New Year's Day 1651. A Scottish army invaded England in support of Charles, but was defeated at the Battle of Worcester in September 1651, after which the king fled to the Continent.

Meanwhile, Oliver Cromwell's forces had also defeated a Scots army at the Battle of Dunbar in September 1650, and following this victory he took Edinburgh. After the restoration of Charles II in 1660, the Scottish Parliament met in 1661 and 1662, passing laws against Presbyterianism and persecuting Covenanters until the end of Charles's reign in 1685.

In 1670, the 71-year-old Major Thomas Weir, a 'Bowhead Saint' (a Calvinist zealot, who lived in the street known as the West Bow), became ill and confessed to practising witchcraft, as well as conducting an incestuous relationship with his unmarried sister Jean (known as 'Grizel'). Weir's sister also confessed, saying that her brother derived his power from his walking stick, which he would send on errands for him.

Old West Bow, late nineteenth century. From Edinburgh and its Environs *(Valentine & Sons, c.1901).*

Despite their far-fetched confessions, Weir and his sister were tried and found guilty. He was strangled and then burned at the stake in Leith Walk (then a country road) on the site of the future tram (and later bus) depot at Shrubhill, while Grizel was hanged in the Grassmarket.

The Duke of York (later James VII of Scotland and II of England), his wife Mary of Modena and daughter Anne lived in Edinburgh from 1679-1682, and were well received by the local populace. When the Duke became king in 1685, he took Roman Catholics under his protection and gave them the Chapel Royal of Holyrood Abbey for their use.

When William of Orange landed in England in 1688, Presbyterians flooded to Edinburgh and a mob attacked and demolished the Chapel Royal, despite being fired on by a guard of about 100 men loyal to James. In something of a frenzy, the mob destroyed Holyrood Abbey and sacked other Catholic chapels and private houses.

At the end of the seventeenth century, William Paterson, founder of the Bank of England, promoted a plan for a Scottish colony at Darien on the Isthmus of Panama. About £400,000 (equivalent to hundreds of millions of pounds today) had been raised in Scotland by public investment as subscriptions to enable a company to trade with India and Africa, as a rival to the English East India Company. All the money was put into the Darien scheme, however.

Five ships sailed from Leith in July 1698, carrying about 1,200 people and landed at Darien in early November. The settlers named their new home 'Caledonia' and began the construction of a town called 'New Edinburgh'. Several more ships arrived in 1699 with an additional 1,300 settlers. Nonetheless, the Darien enterprise proved a disaster, owing to disease, difficulties in trading with the native peoples and with passing ships, lack of support from English colonies (which had been forbidden by William III from assisting the new settlers with food or medications) and attack by the Spaniards, who considered the Darien area part of their empire.

Of the 2,500 settlers, by 1700 only a few hundred had survived, having surrendered to the Spaniards. All the money invested was lost, and many Scots were ruined.

2.5 The eighteenth century: the Union of the Parliaments, the Jacobite rebellions and the Porteous riots

When the people of Edinburgh became aware that the Scottish

Parliament of 1706-1707 was discussing a proposal for union with England, they reacted with suspicion and, when the details of the union were later revealed, they were greatly opposed to it. Crowds of people flocked to the Parliament House and insulted the members of the Scottish Parliament who supported the union. After a mob attacked the home of the Lord Provost, Sir Patrick Johnston, and began roaming the streets, the army was brought in to control the rioters.

Despite the fierce opposition from many Scots, the Union with England Act was passed by 106 votes to 69 (a similar piece of legislation having been passed by the English Parliament in 1706) and the new country of Great Britain came into being on 1 May 1707. England, Scotland and Ireland had been briefly united as one 'Commonwealth' (in effect, a republic) under Oliver Cromwell in June 1657, but this had been dissolved after the death of Cromwell and the Restoration of Charles II to the throne.

Under the 1707 union, Scotland entered into a monetary and customs union with England, but retained her own laws and legal system, with the Church of Scotland remaining as the national church. As a result of the removal of its members of parliament (both lords and commoners, who had sat together in one chamber) to London, Edinburgh was a quieter and less prosperous city for many years.

On the death of the deposed James VII (James II of England) in 1701, his son had declared himself James VIII (James III of England) and in 1715, he landed in Scotland to lead his supporters in a rebellion that was already underway. The Jacobite rebels, although successful further north, failed in their attempt to take Edinburgh Castle. They retreated northwards, and James returned to the Continent from Montrose on 5 February 1716. Later, a serious fire in the Lawnmarket in 1725 caused what the New Statistical Account describes as 'considerable loss of property'.

Another notable event in the city's eighteenth century history occurred in 1736 when two smugglers, Andrew Wilson and George Robertson, were sentenced to be hanged for robbing the collector of excise at Pittenweem in Fife. They tried to escape from the Tolbooth prison, but were unsuccessful as Wilson was too fat to climb out through their cell window, after the two men removed a bar from it. As Wilson had tried to get through the window first, he prevented Robertson from escaping when he became stuck. To make amends for this failure, after

The Old Tolbooth, eighteenth century. From Robert Chambers, Traditions of Edinburgh *(W&R Chambers, 1868, reprinted 1931).*

the Sunday service at the Tolbooth church, Wilson grabbed two of their four guards by the hand and gripped a third with his teeth! Robertson promptly knocked down the fourth guard and escaped.

This act made Wilson something of a hero among the people, so the magistrates armed the Town Guard, led by Captain John Porteous, in case of a rescue attempt. After Wilson's execution on 14 April, the

Edinburgh mob threw stones at the hangman and the guard. Porteous ordered his men to fire above the heads of the mob, but in doing so they shot and wounded people watching from the windows of the houses nearby. The mob became more riotous and Porteous then instructed the Town Guard to fire into the crowds, which caused the deaths of six people and the wounding of eleven others.

Captain Porteous was then tried at the High Court on 5 July, found guilty of murder and sentenced to death on 8 September. Meanwhile, he was imprisoned in the Tolbooth. Porteous's hanging was postponed, and the people of Edinburgh were afraid that he would be pardoned. To ensure that he received his sentence, on 7 September a crowd of about 4,000 stormed the Tolbooth, dragged Porteous from his cell, carried him to the Grassmarket and hanged him from a dyer's pole opposite the Gallows Stone. In consequence, the city was fined £2,000, which was paid to Porteous's widow, and the Lord Provost, Alexander Wilson, was disbarred from all public offices.

In July 1745, Prince Charles Edward Stuart (better known as 'Bonnie Prince Charlie'), the son of 'James VIII (and III of England)', landed in north-west Scotland to raise a Jacobite army and claim the throne for his father, who had named his son as regent. In August, Sir John Cope led the Government troops from Edinburgh to stop the Jacobites, but the Prince and the Highlanders he had raised made for Edinburgh via Perth. When the Jacobites arrived at Corstorphine, then a country village (see Chapter 6.4), the volunteers and militia who were supposed to defend Edinburgh fled in panic.

Early on the morning of 16 September, a party of eighty-four Highlanders was able to rush in at the Netherbow gate (where the High Street meets the Canongate) and seize the city. The Prince then entered Holyrood Palace, where his father was proclaimed king and Charles as his regent. A few days later, the Jacobite army defeated Cope at the Battle of Prestonpans, after which the Prince returned to Holyrood, before leading his army to England and then to his final defeat at Culloden in April 1746. During the Jacobite occupation of Edinburgh, the castle remained in the hands of the Government.

2.6 Outbreaks of plague

At the beginning of August 1348, the plague known as the 'Black Death' entered England via the town of Melcombe Regis (now part of

Weymouth) in Dorset. There had been earlier incidences of plague in Britain, for instance the Britons may have been weakened by the effects of the pandemic known as the Plague of Justinian (then the Eastern Roman Emperor), which took place in 541/542, contributing to their defeat during the Anglo-Saxon invasions.

The Black Death spread rapidly across the south of England, reaching London by the autumn of 1348 and York by the following May. The disease, which seems to have been a particularly virulent combination of bubonic and pneumonic plague, reached what is now the Scottish Borders area in autumn 1349, and was widespread throughout Scotland in 1350. There is no record of how the Black Death affected Edinburgh, but if its consequences were similar to those in England, then between a third and a half of the city's population is likely to have died from the disease.

According to Charles Creighton's *History of Epidemics in Britain*, there were further outbreaks of pestilence in Scotland in 1361/62, 1380, 1392, 1401/02, possibly 1430/31, 1439 (accompanied by famine), 1455, 1475 (with a quarantine station established on Inch Keith in the Firth of Forth), 1495/96, 1497 (an outbreak of syphilis), 1499/1500, 1514/15, 1530, 1539, 1545/46 and 1548.

One of the worst outbreaks of plague in Edinburgh occurred in 1568/69, when around 2,500 people are said to have died. It was the custom at that time to force families with plague to move, with all their belongings, to temporary huts on the Borough Muir, where attempts were made to cleanse their clothes in cauldrons of boiling water on the south bank of the Borough Loch. (Today, the only remaining part of the muir (or moor) not built on is Bruntsfield Links, while the site of the former loch is now the open space known as 'The Meadows'.)

The plague returned in 1574, 1584-1588 (several outbreaks), 1602, 1604-1609 (a number of outbreaks), 1624, and 1644-1648 (when plague victims were housed within huts in Holyrood Park). After this last outbreak, which was particularly bad, plague did not occur again in Scotland, although there were subsequent outbreaks in England.

2.7 Other epidemics

Although the plague did not recur, there were, however, serious epidemics of other diseases in Edinburgh, including cholera, smallpox, influenza, typhus and various fevers. The years 1693-1699 were known as 'the seven ill years': a time of bad harvests, famine and fevers (in particular what was then called 'spotted fever'). The harvest failed in 1782, and Creighton notes that 'the Glasgow and Edinburgh municipalities imported grain for the public benefit.'

In Edinburgh during the winter of 1731/1732 there were outbreaks of what were termed 'worm fever', 'comatose fever' and 'convulsive fever', particularly among children. From October 1735 until February 1736, there was an occurrence of relapsing fever, a disease that is spread by lice and ticks, and caught by people living in insanitary conditions.

Of the 3,110 Edinburgh people who caught the disease in a later outbreak between 1817 and 1819, 138 died. A further epidemic struck in 1827/1828, when, according to the *Edinburgh Medical Journal*:

'It prevailed only among the working classes and the unemployed poor – in the Fountainbridge and West Port districts, the Grassmarket 'closes', the Cowgate and the narrow 'wynds' descending on either side of the long sloping back of the High Street and Canongate.'

In 1832, Edinburgh was hit by an epidemic of cholera which had swept across Europe, with 1,886 cases and 1,065 deaths. Three times as many deaths were reported in Glasgow, although the city's population was only one and a half times as big as that of Edinburgh. Within the suburbs of Edinburgh, however, there were also 267 deaths in Leith, 52 in Newhaven, 33 in Portobello, and 146 in the other suburbs. In addition, 202 people died in Musselburgh and Fisherrow, where the disease had struck before reaching Edinburgh.

Cholera returned in 1848/1849 (with 801 cases and 478 deaths in Edinburgh, 185 in Leith and 20 in Newhaven), in 1853/1854 (with 243 cases and 117 deaths in Edinburgh alone) and in 1866 (with 154 deaths in Edinburgh and 95 in Leith).

A typhus epidemic broke out in Scotland from 1836-1839. In Edinburgh, within fifteen months during 1838/1839, 276 people died out of 2,037 who contracted the disease. Relapsing fever, too, returned to Scotland from 1842-1844, and struck Edinburgh from February 1843 to April 1844. There were about 9,000 cases of the disease in the city, and again the outbreak was confined to 'the poorest and most wretched of the population'.

Charles Creighton states that there were 274 and 206 smallpox deaths in Edinburgh in 1740 and 1741 respectively. He quotes figures showing that, between 1744 and 1763 inclusive, 2,441 Edinburgh citizens died of smallpox, of a total of 24,322 deaths in that period. There were larger scale outbreaks of the disease in 1817 and 1830/1831. More recently, a ship from Bombay brought smallpox to Glasgow when it arrived in the city in May 1942. The disease spread to Edinburgh, where there was a relatively small outbreak with thirty-six cases and eight deaths.

There were also outbreaks of measles in Edinburgh in 1735, 1740/1741 (with 112 deaths) and 1808; whooping cough in 1740/1741 (with 101 deaths). Scarlet fever occurred among the boys of Heriot's Hospital in 1804 and in the city generally in 1805, then again in 1832/1833. Dysentery became rife in 1734, and again in 1828, while enteric or typhoid fever also gained a foothold in 1828 'among the richer classes in the New Town'.

The name 'influenza' comes from the Italian word for 'influence', as the disease was once thought to be caused by the influence of the stars. It was first named influenza within a medical paper written in 1703, and the term has been used in Britain to describe the disease since 1743. Prior to that, various other names were prevalent, such as 'ague'.

Influenza epidemics occurred in Edinburgh in 1733 (but did not affect the prisoners in the gaol, nor the boys in Heriot's Hospital), 1743, 1758 and 1775. From 1889-1892, there was an influenza pandemic. This is believed to have given immunity to older people who lived through the great influenza pandemic of 1918, which is estimated to have killed between 50,000,000 and 100,000,000 people worldwide.

Chapter 3

THE NEW TOWN

3.1 Plans to extend Edinburgh to the north of the castle and the Old Town

In 1726, Daniel Defoe wrote very perceptively in his *Tour Through the Whole Island of Great Britain* that:

'Were not the north side of the hill, which the city [of Edinburgh] stands on, so exceeding steep … and were the lough filled up, as it might easily be, the city might have been extended upon the plain below, and fine beautiful streets would, no doubt, have been built there; nay, I question much whether, in time, the high streets would not have been forsaken, and the city, as we might say, run all out of its gates to the north.'

Defoe was not the only person to believe that Edinburgh was constrained by its location on the slope between the castle and the palace. George Drummond, six times Lord Provost of Edinburgh, threw his civic weight behind the creation of a 'New Town' to the north of the existing city.

In 1765, a contract was signed for a 'North Bridge' to run from the High Street over the end of the Nor' Loch to the ridge beyond. Originally a marshy area, the loch was created in the fifteenth century by the damming of a small river which ran north of the Castle Rock. Drainage of the loch began in the 1760s and continued until the early nineteenth century. The loch area is now East and West Princes Street Gardens, through which the main railway line from Edinburgh to Glasgow runs.

In January 1766, a competition was announced offering entrants the chance to design the layout of the proposed New Town to be built on the north side of the loch, and six designs were entered. The winner was a young Edinburgh architect, the 26-year-old James Craig, whose original proposal was for a layout resembling the union flag. Craig's design had three streets running from east to west, two streets crossing them diagonally, five streets running from north to south, and a square in the middle. (You can see what Craig's design would have looked like on John Laurie's 1766 'Plan of Edinburgh and Places Adjacent', which you can view in the maps and plans section of the National Library of Scotland website: http://maps.nls.uk.)

The boundary of Edinburgh was extended in May 1767 to include within the city the part of St Cuthbert's parish on which the New Town was to be built, and in June of that year, James Craig was awarded a gold medal and the Freedom of the City.

3.2 The First New Town

Craig's union-flag design was not considered suitable for building by Edinburgh's town council and was revised by Craig in 1767 to produce the street plan that still exists today: a simple grid of three streets running from east to west (the present Queen Street, George Street and

Princes Street, East End, early twentieth century. From Edinburgh and its Environs *(Valentine & Sons, c.1901).*

Princes Street – which was originally named St Giles Street), crossed at right angles by three other streets (Castle Street, Frederick Street and Hanover Street) and a square at either end (Charlotte Square – originally called St George's Square – and St Andrew's Square). Two further streets, running east to west between Queen Street and George Street and between the latter and Princes Street, were named Thistle Street and Rose Street. These were to be mews lanes serving the houses in the main streets.

The first buildings in the New Town were at the east end of Thistle Street and in St Andrew's Square. Craig had envisaged that a church would be built in each of the squares, with a view along George Street. The owner of the land, Sir Lawrence Dundas, however, decided that he would place his own home on the site earmarked for St Andrew's Church, which had to be built in George Street instead. Dundas House was built in 1774, then purchased by the Royal Bank of Scotland in 1821 to be the bank's headquarters.

The construction of Charlotte Square, which began in 1792 and was finished in 1820, saw the completion of what later became known as the First New Town. There had been public criticism of the town council for the piecemeal way in which the New Town had been developed, and so the council commissioned the architect Robert Adam in 1791, to design Charlotte Square as a whole.

The central part of the north side of the square was bought in 1806 by Sir John Sinclair of Ulbster, the originator of the Statistical Accounts of Scotland (see Chapter 17). After having passed through a number of owners, the house came into the possession of John Crichton-Stuart, the 4th Marquess of Bute, in the early twentieth century and was named Bute House. The house was given to the National Trust for Scotland by the 6th Marquis of Bute in 1966 and, after being refurbished, it became the Edinburgh residence of the Secretary of State for Scotland.

Since 1999, Bute House has been the official residence of the First Minister of the devolved Scottish Government, and it functions in a similar way to 10 Downing Street for the Prime Minister of the United Kingdom.

Next door to Bute House, at Number 7, Charlotte Square, is the National Trust for Scotland's 'Georgian House', which is open to the public. John Lamont, 18th Chief of Clan Lamont, lived there with his family from 1796-1815. The house was restored in the 1970s to show a typical New Town home of the late eighteenth and early nineteenth centuries.

George Street was originally meant to be the main street in the New Town, but it was eclipsed by Princes Street as more and more shops began to be opened there. This continued in the nineteenth and twentieth centuries, as much larger shop buildings replaced Princes Street's original private houses.

Princes Street, looking towards the West End, early twentieth century. From Edinburgh and its Environs *(Valentine & Sons, c.1901).*

According to Michael Fry's *Edinburgh: A History of the City*, the Edinburgh town council's plans to build on the south (gardens) side of Princes Street were halted in 1772, when a case brought by the owners of the north side of the street was decided in the House of Lords against the council. Fry makes the point that this was only possible because of Scotland's continued use of the feudal system until 2004. Under this system, the owners of the buildings on the north side of Princes Street were not freeholders (as they would have been in England) but feuars, i.e. holders of feu-charters from a feudal superior, in this case from the town council.

The feuars argued successfully that their charters were based on James Craig's plan for the New Town, which quite clearly showed gardens (and a canal in the place of the Nor' Loch) on the opposite side of the street.

3.3 The Second and subsequent New Towns
The first phase of the New Town was such a success that it was decided in the early nineteenth century to extend it downhill to the north of Queen Street Gardens. This Northern New Town (as far north as Fettes Lane and Royal Crescent), planned by Robert Reid and William Sibbald, included some curved terraces (such as Abercromby Place, Drummond Place and Royal Circus), breaking away from the rectangular plan of the First New Town.

A further extension of the New Town followed to the west, in accordance with a master plan drawn up around 1813 by James Gillespie (later known as James Gillespie Graham after his second marriage). This Third New Town (the West End) was bounded by Shandwick Place, Queensferry Street, Belford Road, Magdala Crescent and Haymarket Terrace.

To the east of the First New Town, a new bridge was constructed in what was named Waterloo Place between 1815 and 1819, leading from Princes Street to Calton Prison and crossing Calton Road, which led from Holyrood to the top of Leith Walk. A new road, named Regent Road, joined Waterloo Place to the existing road from Portobello.

In 1818, William Henry Playfair was appointed to design an eastern Fourth New Town (the Calton New Town) around the lower slopes of the Calton Hill. His design has Royal Terrace facing the north and Regent Terrace the south-east (with a large private garden behind them) and Carlton Terrace linking the other two terraces.

On the other side of the new London Road (connecting Leith Walk and the continuation of Regent Road), Hillside Crescent was built, with three streets leading off it and two off London Road. It had originally

Leith Walk, early nineteenth century. From Robert Chambers, Traditions of Edinburgh *(W & R Chambers, 1868; reprinted 1931).*

been proposed to build the Calton New Town between Leith Walk and Lochend Road almost as far as Duke Street, on land belonging to Heriot's and Trinity Hospitals. Planned new streets included Heriot Crescent (off Leith Walk, opposite the existing Pilrig Street), Trinity Square (roughly where Dalmeny Park is today) and Playfair Street (near the present Brunswick Road, but on a different alignment). This development never happened, though.

In 1782, the Earl of Moray bought a piece of land to the north of the future Charlotte Square: the Drumsheugh Estate. Drumsheugh House was situated on the south-east of the present Randolph Crescent. The estate was bounded by the First New Town to the south, the Second to the east, the Third to the west, and the Water of Leith to the north. The next Earl decided in 1822 to demolish Drumsheugh House and build houses on the estate, and he commissioned Gillespie to produce a plan. The new streets in the development of this Fifth New Town included the circular Moray Place (with a 3.5 acre central private garden) and Ainslie Place, as well as Randolph Crescent, linking the earlier New Town areas. The Earl of Moray reserved the very grand Number 28, Moray Place for himself.

In 1995, the Old and New Towns of Edinburgh were declared a World Heritage Site by UNESCO (the United Nations Educational,

Scientific and Cultural Organisation) for their 'remarkable blend of the urban phenomena of organic medieval growth and eighteenth and nineteenth century town planning.'

3.4 The Scottish Enlightenment

In the eighteenth and early nineteenth centuries, the Scottish Enlightenment contributed to the general European 'Age of Enlightenment' – with an emphasis on reason, analysis and individualism, rather than a blind acceptance of tradition. Many ideas that we take for granted nowadays originated during the period of the Enlightenment.

Perhaps in part filling the vacuum caused by the departure from Edinburgh to London of the royal court in 1603 and the Scottish Government in 1707, there was a great flowering of culture (architecture, art, education, literature and philosophy) and science (including technology and social sciences, particularly economics). This was especially noticeable in the royal burghs that were home to Scotland's four early universities: St Andrews, Glasgow, Aberdeen and Edinburgh.

The literary side of the Enlightenment was represented by the poets Robert Burns, Edinburgh-born Robert Fergusson, Allan Ramsay (father of the artist of the same name) and James Thomson, and the novelists Sir Walter Scott (born in Edinburgh) and Tobias Smollett.

Allan Ramsay, the painter (1713-1784). From Francis Watt's Book of Edinburgh Anecdote *(T N Foulis, 1912).*

Sir Walter Scott (1771-1832). From Edinburgh and its Environs *(Valentine & Sons, c.1901).*

The principal artists of the period were Allan Ramsay Junior, Sir Henry Raeburn, Alexander Naysmith and his son Patrick – all born in Edinburgh – and David Allan. In architecture, the leaders were William Adam and his sons John, Robert (designer of the New Town's Charlotte Square) and James, together with Sir William Bruce of Kinross, Colin Campbell, James Gibbs and the Edinburgh-born Robert Mylne.

Foremost among the philosophers of the age was the Edinburgh-born David Hume (originally spelt Home), whose major works (published during the 1740s) were *A Treatise of Human Nature* and *Essays, Moral and Political*. Other important Scottish philosophers included George Campbell, Francis Hutcheson, Thomas Reid and Dugald Stewart (who was also born in Edinburgh).

Adam Smith, known as 'the father of modern economics' and still influential today, was the author of *The Wealth of Nations*, published in 1776, which is considered to be the very first book on economics. Other leading social scientists were Adam Ferguson, John Millar and William Robertson.

Scottish scientists of the period included the chemist and physicist Joseph Black, the Edinburgh-born geologist James Hutton (whose conclusion that Earth was much older than a few thousand years indirectly influenced the work of Charles Darwin on evolution), the mathematicians David Gregory and John Playfair (uncle of William Henry Playfair the architect) and the engineer James Watt.

The figures of the Scottish Enlightenment made a disproportionately large contribution to the science and literature of the British Empire up to the mid-nineteenth century, and their political ideas were an important influence on the founders of the United States of America.

Chapter 4

EDINBURGH IN THE
LAST 200 YEARS

4.1 The Great Fire of Edinburgh

Although Edinburgh had previously been protected by volunteer firemen, the city's first permanent municipal fire brigade (also the first in the UK) was founded in October 1824. This measure was taken just in time to deal with what became known as the 'Great Fire of Edinburgh', which raged in part of the Old Town during mid-November 1824.

The fire started at about 10.00 pm on Monday, 15 November in the workshop of the Kirkwood family of engravers within a tenement building in Old Assembly Close, off the High Street, by Parliament Square. This had also been the scene of a serious fire in 1700.

The new fire brigade promptly responded to the emergency, yet the firemen had difficulty in getting the engines through the narrow closes of the Old Town and in finding water. As a result, the fire had spread to three neighbouring buildings by midnight. One of the buildings affected housed the *Edinburgh Courant* newspaper, which boasted Daniel Defoe among its former editors.

Despite the efforts of the fire brigade and volunteer firemen, more and more buildings caught fire. By noon on the Tuesday, the blaze had advanced east into the High Street, reaching the Tron Church on the corner of the High Street and the South Bridge. After the steeple caught fire, the church bell began to melt and it soon came loose, crashing to the ground below.

On Tuesday evening, with assistance from the military in the castle, the fire brigade seemed to be gradually bringing the blaze under control, when a second fire broke out on the eleventh floor of a building in Parliament Square which overlooked the Cowgate. Again neighbouring buildings caught fire, and efforts were made to stop the fire spreading to St Giles' Church and the law courts. Fortunately, pouring rain on the Wednesday put out the fire, although some of the buildings continued to smoulder until the Friday.

Eleven people had been killed by the fire, including two firemen, and two citizens hit by falling masonry. More than 1,000 people had lost their homes, and they were given temporary accommodation in Queensberry House at the foot of the Canongate. Houses were destroyed in the High Street, Conn's Close, Old Assembly Close, Borthwick's Close, Old Fishmarket Close and Parliament Close.

The 23-year-old James Braidwood, the first Firemaster of the Edinburgh Fire Brigade, left the city to lead what became the London Fire Brigade in 1833. Sadly, he was killed by a falling wall during the Tooley Street Warehouse Fire near London Bridge in 1861. A statue of Braidwood was unveiled in Edinburgh's Parliament Square in 2008.

4.2 Aerial attack during the First World War

A large number of Edinburgh men fought in the First World War, but from 11.25 pm on Sunday, 2 April 1916 to 12.25 am on Monday, 3 April, the war came to Edinburgh. During those 60 minutes, the city suffered an aerial bombardment of explosive and incendiary bombs from a German airship, Zeppelin L14. Compared to other towns and cities Edinburgh got off very lightly, but nevertheless, thirteen people were killed and twenty-four were injured in the attack.

The target of the raid was the naval base at Rosyth, a short distance away up the Firth of Forth, but the airship captain couldn't find it and dropped his bombs on Leith and Edinburgh instead. As the authorities had received advance warning of a likely attack, the traffic had been stopped and all lights put out. The Central Fire Station, Red Cross and Police Headquarters had been notified, with all off-duty regular and special police called out.

The first bombs caused damage but no injuries. The fifth (explosive) bomb, however, landed on the roof of 2 Commercial Street in Leith, killing the 66-year-old man who lived on the top floor of the building. Meanwhile, at 14 Commercial Street an incendiary bomb fell through the roof and then straight through the floor into the flat below, where it burst into flames. The old woman who lived on the top floor reportedly got out of bed quite calmly and poured water through the hole in the floor, extinguishing the fire.

Another explosive bomb struck the bonded warehouse of Innes & Grieve, wholesale spirit merchants in Leith. Casks of whisky exploded in the streets, and local people rushed to collect it in bottles and jugs or even their bare hands! The firm put in a claim to the British Government for £99,000 worth of damage, but received only half of that amount.

One of the airship's incendiary bombs also crashed through the roof of a tenement at 15 Church Street, Leith, and again went straight through the floor. The upper floor housed the wife of a soldier and her three children, while a married couple with five children lived on the floor below. Although both floors were set alight and much damage was done, none of the occupants were injured.

In Mill Lane, on the other side of the Water of Leith, the manse of St Thomas's Church was struck by one of the incendiary bombs and immediately went up in flames. Although the building was almost destroyed, the minister, his wife and servant, who had been asleep, were uninjured. Not everyone was so lucky. A one-year-old baby was killed when a fragment of shell came through a window, after an explosive bomb landed in a courtyard at 200 Bonnington Road.

After bombing Leith, the airship moved on to Edinburgh, where an explosive bomb landed on vacant ground at Bellevue Terrace at 11.50 pm, followed by an incendiary on the roadway at the Mound. At 39 Lauriston Place (the home of a Dr John McLaren), the roof, ceiling and party wall were all damaged by an explosive bomb. No-one was hurt inside the building, yet a man outside in the street about 80 yards away in Graham Street was injured and later died.

The next explosive bomb fell in the grounds of George Watson's College (with no resulting injuries); an incendiary landed in the Meadows; and, at about 11.55 pm, an explosive bomb struck numbers 80 and 82 Marchmont Crescent. Again, part of the shell passed through the upper storeys to the ground floor, and again, no-one was injured.

At 183 Causewayside, however, where the next explosive bomb fell, six people were injured, including a 71-year-old woman who died later, and the building was 'practically wrecked', as the police report noted. Incendiary bombs were subsequently dropped in the back gardens of houses at 81 Hatton Place and 28 Blacket Place, but caused no damage.

The airship then turned back towards the city centre, releasing an incendiary in the grounds of the Royal Infirmary. An explosive bomb fell in the Grassmarket, opposite the White Hart Hotel, where four people were injured, one of whom later died. The next explosive bomb fell on the south-west corner of the Castle Rock.

A guest at Brown's County Hotel (later part of the rebuilt Caley Cinema) in Lothian Road was slightly injured when the hotel was struck by an explosive bomb, severely damaging the roof and the interior of the building. Three explosive bombs were then dropped at different points in the Water of Leith valley.

By this time the city had been awakened by the explosions, and many people had come outside to see the airship. At about 12.20 am, six bystanders were killed and seven injured, when an explosive bomb landed on the pavement outside 16 Marshall Street. Three people were injured by an explosive bomb at Haddon's Court, Nicolson Street, and at 69 St Leonard's Hill a child was killed and two people were injured, also by an explosive bomb.

An incendiary and three explosive bombs were dropped in Holyrood Park, as well as an incendiary in the grounds of Prestonfield House, before the airship left the Edinburgh area at about 12.25 am. Although we now know that no further air raids on Edinburgh took place during the First World War, in 1916 many citizens feared further attacks.

4.3 The Edinburgh Festival and Fringe

On 24 August 1947, the first Edinburgh International Festival (EIF) of Music and Drama took place, opening with a Service of Praise and Thanksgiving in St Giles' Church. The Third Statistical Account of Edinburgh relates that:

> 'The Glyndebourne Opera performed *The Marriage of Figaro* and Verdi's Macbeth. Concerts were given by the Vienna Philharmonic Orchestra under Bruno Walter … with Kathleen Ferrier … l'Orchestre des Concerts Colonne under Paul Paray, the Hallé Orchestra under Barbirolli, the Liverpool Philharmonic under Sargent, and the Scottish National and BBC Scottish Orchestras under Walter Susskind and Ian Whyte.
>
> 'Drama was represented by the Old Vic company in *The Taming of the Shrew* and, with Alec Guinness, in *Richard II* … The Sadler's Wells Ballet with Margot Fonteyn performed Tchaikovsky's *The Sleeping Beauty*.'

Traverse Theatre, 2011 by Kim Traynor. (Available under a Creative Commons Attribution-Share Alike 3.0 Unported licence at http://commons.wikimedia.org/wiki/File:Traverse_Theatre,_Edinburgh.jpg)

'An encouraging start', reported the Statistical Account with some understatement.

Most of the performances at the EIF are what some people would term 'highbrow', but several other festivals also take place in Edinburgh as well as the 'official' festival. Even in 1947, there were many other 'unofficial' performances. Eight theatre groups had arrived in Edinburgh uninvited, and had simply put on their shows on the 'fringe' of the 'official' festival.

In 1958, the Festival Fringe Society was created to: formalise the existence of these 'fringe' shows, provide information to artists, publish a programme of performances, and establish a central booking office. The Fringe has grown over the years to become what the Society calls 'the world's largest arts festival', which 'includes anyone with a story to tell and a venue willing to host them'.

Festivals Edinburgh was established in 2007 by the directors of the twelve leading festivals, amongst which are the:

Festival theatre, Nicholson Street, 2006. (Available under a Creative Commons Attribution-Share Alike 3.0 Unported licence at http://commons.wikimedia.org/wiki/File:Festival_Theatre.jpg)

- **Edinburgh International Science Festival** (founded in 1988), a two-week event which takes place in April;
- **Imaginate Festival** (founded in 1990), an international festival of performing arts for children and young people in May;
- **Edinburgh International Film Festival** (founded in 1947), held in June;
- **Edinburgh Jazz and Blues Festival** (founded in 1978), organised each July;
- **Edinburgh Art Festival** (founded in 2004), which runs from the end of July until the end of August;
- **Royal Edinburgh Military Tattoo** (founded in 1950), with massed bands and other performers, stretches over three weeks in August;
- **Edinburgh International Festival** (the 'official' festival, founded in 1947), which takes place around the same three weeks as the Tattoo, but lasts slightly longer;
- **Edinburgh Festival Fringe** (also founded in 1947), occurs at the same time as the 'official' festival;
- **Edinburgh International Book Festival** (founded in 1983), is located in Charlotte Square Gardens over the last two weeks of the 'official' festival;
- **Edinburgh Mela** ('Scotland's biggest celebration of world music and dance', founded in 1995), is held over two days at the end of August;
- **Scottish International Storytelling Festival** (founded in 1990), takes place during the last week in October;
- **Edinburgh's Hogmanay** (founded in 1994), is celebrated over three days around Hogmanay (New Year's Eve).

4.4 City of Literature

In 2004, the United Nations Educational, Scientific and Cultural Organisation (UNESCO) launched a Creative Cities Network to connect cities eager 'to share experiences, ideas and best practices for cultural, social and economic development.' The network includes Cities of Literature, Film, Music, Crafts and Folk Art, Design, Media Arts and Gastronomy.

In the network's founding year, Edinburgh became the first City of Literature. According to the City of Literature website, www.cityof literature.com:

'In 2002, Edinburgh was a literary powerhouse, attracting and spawning best-selling writers, home to vibrant publishing houses and the birthplace of the world's biggest book festival. Then as now, Edinburgh was bursting with literary history and heritage, and four book lovers – James Boyle, Jenny Brown, Lorraine Fannin and Catherine Lockerbie – decided over an extended lunch to approach UNESCO to recognise the rich past, innovative present and potential future of Edinburgh as a City of Literature.'

James Boyle is the current Chairman of the National Library of Scotland, and Chairman of the British Council in Scotland (and he was formerly Chairman of the Scottish Arts Council, Chairman of the Scottish Government's Cultural Commission, Controller of BBC Radio Four, and Head of BBC Radio Scotland).

Jenny Brown is an Edinburgh literary agent, and Chair of the Bloody Scotland crime writing festival. She was previously Head of Literature at the Scottish Arts Council, presenter of book programmes for Scottish Television, and founder Director of the Edinburgh International Book Festival.

Lorraine Fannin is a Trustee of the National Library of Scotland and a consultant for the Scottish Centre for the Book at Edinburgh Napier University (see Chapter 16.3), where she is also a guest lecturer. She was formerly Director of the Scottish Publishers' Association (SPA) and Chief Executive of Publishing Scotland (the successor organisation to the SPA) for over twenty years. She was also a member of the British Council Publishers' Advisory Committee, the Publishing Qualifications Board and the Institute of Publishing Advisory Board.

Catherine Lockerbie was   Literary Editor of *The Scotsman* and Director of the Edinburgh International Book Festival for nearly ten years. She has been a judge for literary prizes, including the Whitbread Book Awards (now the Costa Book Awards) and the Orange Prize for Fiction (now the Baileys Women's Prize for Fiction).

Since 2004, six other cities around the world have become Cities of Literature: Melbourne (2008); Iowa City (2008); Dublin (2010); Reykjavik (2011); Norwich (2012) and Krakow (2013).

4.5 The devolved Scottish Government

From 1707-1999, Scotland was governed from London, and during this time Edinburgh lost much of its importance as the capital of Scotland. In the twentieth century 'home rule' for Scotland was advocated by many people, such as the Scottish Covenant Association. The 1949 Scottish Covenant received about 2,000,000 signatures (out of a population of just over 5,000,000) in favour of devolution.

Despite the Scottish Covenant, nothing was done until the Royal Commission on the Constitution (chaired initially by Lord Crowther, and then by Lord Kilbrandon) reported in 1973. The Kilbrandon Report advocated devolved assemblies for Scotland and Wales, as well as eight regional assemblies for England.

Under the UK Labour Government's Scotland Act of 1978, a referendum was held on Scottish devolution in 1979, under which more than 40 per cent of the electorate had to be in favour for the proposition to be carried. Although 51.6 per cent of those who voted were in favour, this amounted to only 32.9 per cent of the Scottish electorate.

Nearly twenty years passed before the next devolution referendum was held by the new UK Labour Government. In 1997, 74.29 per cent voted in favour of a devolved Scottish Parliament and 63.48 per cent agreed that it should have tax-varying powers. Accordingly, the Scotland Act of 1998 created a devolved Scottish Parliament, which first met on 12 May 1999.

The old Parliament House in use up to 1707 then became the home of the Court of Session and so could not house the new parliament. It had been intended that the main hall of the former Royal High School would become the new Parliament House, and it was refurbished accordingly. The new Scottish Parliament did not move into the old High School, however, and in June 1999 construction began of a new parliament building in Edinburgh at Holyrood, designed by a Catalan architect, Enric Miralles. The first debate took place there on 7 September 2004.

The first election in 1999 produced a Scottish Government (at that time known as the 'Scottish Executive') that was a coalition of Labour and Liberal Democrat members, led by the former UK Scottish Secretary Donald Dewar as First Minister. After Dewar's death in October 2000, the coalition was led by Henry McLeish, who was succeeded by Jack McConnell in November 2001.

Following the Scottish Parliament election of 2007, a minority government was formed by Alex Salmond, leader of the Scottish National Party (SNP), which had won forty-seven of the one hundred and twenty-nine seats (Labour had won forty-six). At the next Scottish Parliament election in 2011, the SNP increased its number of seats to sixty-nine (while Labour dropped to thirty-seven), allowing the SNP to form a majority government. The SNP advocates complete

Main Chamber of the Scottish Parliament, 2007 by Martyn Gorman. (Available under a Creative Commons Attribution-Share Alike 2.0 Generic licence at http://commons. wikimedia.org/wiki/File:The_main_chamber_the_Scottish_Parliament_-_geograph.org. uk_-_400523.jpg)

Scottish Parliament Building, 2006. (Available under a Creative Commons Attribution-Share Alike 3.0 Unported licence at http://commons.wikimedia.org/wiki/File:Edinburgh _Scottish_Parliament01_2006-04-29.jpg)

independence for Scotland, and negotiated with the UK Government to hold an independence referendum in September 2014.

The result of the referendum was that 55 per cent of those voting (on a voter turnout of 85 per cent of the electorate) wished Scotland to stay in the UK, while 45 per cent preferred an independent Scotland. (In Edinburgh, 61 per cent voted 'no' to independence, whereas in Glasgow, 54 per cent voted 'yes'.) Shortly before the referendum vote, the three main UK political parties had pledged to give the Scottish Parliament 'extensive new powers'.

4.6 Edinburgh's trades and industries

Edinburgh is the biggest financial centre in the UK after London, and has been a major banking centre since the Bank of Scotland (now part of the Lloyds Banking Group) was founded in 1695. The Bank of

Scotland's headquarters are in Edinburgh, as are those of the Royal Bank of Scotland, which was established in 1727.

Major Edinburgh insurance companies include Standard Life, founded in 1825, and Scottish Widows, founded in 1815. These two companies are now located in the city's new Exchange financial district, which also contains the Edinburgh International Conference Centre.

Being the location of the main Scottish law courts (see Chapter 13), Edinburgh is the centre of Scotland's legal profession. The city is also a major educational hub, with four universities (see Chapter 16) in addition to many state and independent schools (see Chapter 15).

According to *Bartholomew's Survey Gazetteer of the British Isles*, in 1904:

> 'The principal industries of Edinburgh are printing, type-founding, bookbinding, lithographing and engraving; machine-making and brass-founding; coach-building; manufactures of glass and jewellery; tanning, brewing and distilling. There are four distilleries.
>
> 'Edinburgh has long been famous for its medical schools, which have attracted students from all parts of the world.'

4.7 Edinburgh's football teams

Edinburgh has two professional football clubs: Heart of Midlothian FC (known as 'Hearts') and Hibernian FC (known as 'Hibs').

Hearts was founded in 1874 by members of the Heart of Midlothian Dancing Club, and the team first played matches at the East Meadows, Powburn and Powderhall, before moving to Gorgie in 1881. The team has played at Tynecastle Stadium in Gorgie since 1886, when it leased the ground from Edinburgh Corporation, before buying it in 1926.

Hearts have won the Scottish League Championship four times (the last time being in 1960); they have been runners-up fourteen times (most recently in 2006), and have come third seventeen times, (the last occasion being in 2011). The team have also won the Scottish Cup on eight occasions (with their last victory in 2012), and they have been runners-up on six (most recently in 1996). Hearts have won the Scottish League Cup on four occasions (lastly in 1962), and they have been runners-up three times, most recently in 2013.

In 1875, Hearts' great rival team Hibs was founded. Hibernian FC was established by Irish immigrants, hence the name and the team's green jerseys (Hearts wear a maroon kit). Hibs have played at Easter Road Stadium since 1893, having previously occupied the Meadows and Hibernian Park (near Easter Road, and now covered by Bothwell Street).

Hibs have won the Scottish League Championship four times (most recently in 1952), and they were runners-up on six occasions (the last being in 1975). The team has also won the Scottish Cup in 1887 and 1902, having been runners-up on eleven occasions (the most recent in 2013). Hibs were the victors in the Scottish League Cup in 1972, 1991 and 2007, and runners-up on six occasions (the last in 2004).

4.8 Transport in Edinburgh

On Monday, 16 November 1871, Edinburgh's first tramway service was opened, running on rails in the roadway from Bernard Street in Leith via Leith Walk and Princes Street to the Haymarket.

The Edinburgh Street Tramways Company had been authorised by the Edinburgh Tramways Act of 1871 to build routes in Edinburgh, Leith and Portobello. The earliest trams were horse-drawn, as were the buses of the time, but from 1881-1882 steam trams were tested out on the Edinburgh to Portobello line. However, they were discontinued because of public complaints about the smoke and noise.

In 1884, a cable tramway system was opened from Hanover Street in the New Town to Goldenacre down the steep gradient to the north. The cable system was similar to the one still in use today in San Francisco, where the cars are pulled by a cable running continuously under the street held by a 'grip' attached to the car. When the trams need to stop, the grip is simply released from the cable.

In 1892, Edinburgh Corporation compulsorily purchased the part of the tramway system that ran within the city's boundaries, while the tram company continued to operate services in Leith and Portobello. This meant that passengers travelling from Princes Street to the foot of Leith Walk had to change trams halfway down Leith Walk at Pilrig Street, which was on the boundary of Edinburgh and Leith. This situation continued for the next thirty years.

Edinburgh had converted all its horse-drawn tram lines to cable by 1907. Leith had begun to use electric trams in 1905, and after the amalgamation of Edinburgh and Leith in 1920, Edinburgh began switching over to an electric tramway system in 1922. Within the same year, a through service from Edinburgh to Leith began operating, and the switchover to electric trams was completed in 1924.

Tramway services for commuters were operated to Edinburgh's growing suburbs, such as Comely Bank, Corstorphine, Stenhouse, Slateford, Colinton, Fairmilehead, Liberton and Portobello. One of the services to Portobello continued beyond the city boundary to Levenhall, at the east end of Musselburgh.

Beginning in 1950, Edinburgh began to replace its tram services with buses. On 16 November 1956, a final fleet of trams made their way down the Mound, where presentations were made to three drivers, then along Princes Street, St Andrew Square, York Place and Leith Walk to the depot at Shrubhill.

As well as its tram services, Edinburgh also had bus services and a suburban rail network, which ran services to Leith, Granton, Davidson's Mains, Barnton, Corstorphine, Slateford, Balerno, Joppa and places farther east. Many of these stations were closed from the 1920s onwards, with Corstorphine Station becoming the last to close in 1967.

Lothian Regional Council put forward plans in 1989 to construct an Edinburgh Metro light rail service, with a north-south line running from Easter Drylaw to Cameron Toll West. From Easter Drylaw, separate lines would travel to Davidson's Mains and Muirhouse, and from Cameron Toll West to Burdiehouse and Gilmerton. From Canonmills to Newington, the line would move underground. An east-west Metro line was envisaged for later implementation, from Leith to Wester Hailes via St Andrew Square and Haymarket.

In addition, it was proposed to re-open the former suburban circular railway line serving Edinburgh's southern suburbs. As well as the existing Waverley and Haymarket stations, possible new stations were planned for Gorgie, Craiglockhart, Morningside, Blackford, Mayfield, Cameron Toll East, Craigmillar, Niddrie, Asda, Portobello, Piershill, Meadowbank and Abbeyhill.

The cost of the north-south Metro line was considered prohibitive, and instead of the east-west line, a guided busway was planned and part of it was built from Gyle to Saughton. In 2005, a referendum was held in Edinburgh to decide whether there should be a 'congestion charge' payable for driving in the city centre, as in London. Around 75 per cent of voters were against the charge, which would have been used

Tram in Princes Street, 2014. (Author's collection)

to help fund a new tramway system proposed by the City of Edinburgh Council, after a public consultation in 2003.

Fifty years after disposing of its trams, Edinburgh Council was proposing to bring them back. A three-line system was planned, with two lines approved by the Scottish Parliament, and one line built from Edinburgh Airport to York Place. Construction of the line began in June 2008, but because of various problems and disputes, the first tram did not run until 31 May 2014.

4.9 Air raids during the Second World War

Despite the far higher number of air raids on Edinburgh during the Second World War than in the First, the number of people killed as a result was still relatively small: eighteen people lost their lives in raids between June 1940 and July 1942. The number injured was 212, much higher than in 1916.

A total of 47 bombs and mines, plus 452 incendiaries, were dropped on Edinburgh on ten occasions in 1940, three in 1941 and one in 1942. The first air raid occurred at about 1.00 am on 26 June 1940, when five bombs and 100 incendiaries were dropped on open ground near Craigmillar Castle Road. In the next raid, the Victoria Dock and railway lines in Leith were targeted with eight bombs just after 8.00 pm on 18 July.

Eight people were killed and thirty-eight injured at about 6.00 am on 22 July, when Leith's Albert Dock was struck by a 1,000lb bomb, and the railway lines nearby at Seafield Road were hit by three small bombs and forty-eight incendiaries. In the same raid, 100 incendiaries rained down on Granton.

At 1.30 am on 4 August, five bombs landed on Portobello at Abercorn Park, Abercorn Terrace, Christian Path, Argyle Place and Argyle Crescent, but fortunately none exploded.

On 27 September, a 500lb bomb was dropped on Duff Street, Gorgie at 5.15 am. According to Alexander Reid's *Aye Ready! The History of Edinburgh Fire Brigade*:

'As a result of the explosion and the fire that followed, a five-storey bonded store belonging to the Distillers Company Limited was wholly destroyed and many tenements in Duff Street, Springwell Place and Downfield Place badly damaged.

'It took 30 [fire] appliances and 138 firemen under the command of Second Officer R. Wylie to deal with this fire, as a result of which 135 families were evacuated and 50 had to be rehoused.

'Among the many odd incidents associated with this fire was one in which a large cask of whisky, blown out of the store by the explosion, crashed through a tenement roof and came to rest on a table, still half full of blazing spirits!'

Subsequently that day, a bomb was dropped in the grounds of Holyrood Palace, leaving a huge crater in the middle of the palace lawn. On the evening of 29 September, a 250lb bomb was dropped on Crewe Place, killing two children: Ronald and Morag MacArthur, aged seven and five years respectively.

On 7 October, five smaller bombs were dropped on Roseneath

Place, Marchmont Crescent, Marchmont Road and Meadow Place in the Warrender Park area, injuring eleven people. Corstorphine was hit by six 250lb bombs in the next attack on 5 November, in which bombs landed on Pinkhill House, on open ground at the Zoo, in Corstorphine Hill quarry and in the grounds of Clermiston House. Both of these air raids took place in the evening.

For four months there were no raids on Edinburgh, with the next taking place at midnight on 14/15 March 1941. That night about seventy incendiaries were dropped on the Abbeyhill area by German aircraft on their way to Glasgow. Two landmines were dropped on Leith by parachute at 11.00 pm on 7 April, killing three people and injuring 131 others when tenements in Largo Place were struck. The infant annexe of David Kilpatrick School was destroyed, and Leith Town Hall was badly damaged, as were 270 houses, 200 shops and three churches.

The last raid in 1941 took place at about 12.30 am on 6 May. Four people were killed and two injured when one 100lb bomb, three smaller bombs and thirty-four incendiaries were dropped on Niddrie Road, Milton Crescent and Jewel Cottages.

Fourteen months passed before the final raid on Edinburgh, at 11.20 pm on 6 July 1942. Four 500lb bombs fell on Craigentinny House, Loaning Road, Loaning Crescent (in this case the bomb did not explode) and Craigentinny Golf Course.

Chapter 5

LEITH, NORTH AND SOUTH

5.1 Edinburgh's seaport from early times

The town of Leith takes its name from the river known as the Water of Leith, and was first documented in 1128 in the charter of Holyrood Abbey. The name 'Leith' is Brythonic (Old Welsh) in origin, according to W J Watson's *Celtic Place-names of Scotland*, and may have the same root as the Welsh word *llaith*, meaning damp or moist.

The river, described as 'a small, sluggish stream, polluted with sewage and the discharge from factories' in the 1885 *Ordnance Gazetteer of Scotland*, divided the area into the parishes of North Leith on the west bank and South Leith on the east. The latter was traditionally known as Restalrig and its feudal superior was the Laird of Restalrig.

Most of the original town of Leith was situated in the large South Leith parish, which extended as far south as Calton Road, Jock's Lodge and the Fishwives' Causeway and as far east as Portobello Harbour, at the mouth of the Figgate Burn. The oldest streets in Leith were the Kirkgate, Tolbooth Wynd and the Shore, on the south bank of the Water of Leith and continued as the Coalhill, (part of North Leith, although on the south bank), Sheriff Brae and Mill Lane. The *Gazetteer* describes these thoroughfares as narrow, dirty and dingy – typical of Leith's Old Town.

Leith's historic function as a port was due to the natural harbour at the mouth of the Water of Leith. All the ships anchored in the harbour were burned by the army of King Edward II of England in 1313, a year before the Battle of Bannockburn took place. The ships in the harbour were again burned by the English in 1410.

In 1329, Robert the Bruce granted the port of Leith and its mills to the burgesses of the city of Edinburgh, and in 1428, James I allowed the city to levy a tax on all ships and boats entering Leith harbour. James II bestowed on Edinburgh in 1454 the customs duties on ships' cargo landed at Leith, and in 1482 James III confirmed this in more detail. In

Leith Shore, 2006. (Available under a Creative Commons Attribution-Share Alike 3.0 Unported licence at http://en.wikipedia.org/wiki/File:LeithView.jpg)

1510, James IV also granted Edinburgh taxation rights to the new port of Newhaven.

Robert Ballantyne, the Abbot of Holyrood, built St Ninian's Chapel (which later became North Leith Church) in 1493, as well as the first bridge across the river connecting North and South Leith. At the southern end of South Leith parish, Restalrig Church in the old village of Restalrig (originally Lestalrig) dates back to at least 1178. St Mary's Chapel in the town of Leith was built about 1483 and became the parish church of South Leith after the Reformation in 1560, being formally confirmed as such in 1609.

In 1544, Leith and all the ships in the harbour were seized by the Earl of Hertford and an army of 10,000 men who plundered the town and the area around it, setting the town on fire before they departed. Three years later, now known as Duke of Somerset, he did the same thing, with less damage caused to Leith this time, but resulting in the loss of thirty-five ships.

South Leith Parish Church, 2010 by Kim Traynor. (Available under a Creative Commons Attribution-Share Alike 3.0 Unported licence at http://en.wikipedia.org/wiki/File:South_Leith_Parish_Kirk.jpg)

A stone wall was built around Leith from 1548-1549, with six gates or 'ports' and a wooden bridge over the Water of Leith. This wall was soon tested. At St Anthony's Port, by the Kirkgate, in 1560 there was fighting between Scottish and French forces in support of the Roman Catholic Queen Regent Mary of Guise (then ruling in the name of her daughter Mary, Queen of Scots), and Scottish and English forces supporting the 'Lords of the Congregation' (Scottish Protestant nobles).

Leith came under siege in April 1560, until after the death of Mary of Guise on 11 June, the Treaty of Edinburgh was signed by the Scots,

English and French. Under the terms of the treaty, the English and French armies withdrew from Scotland.

In 1645, Leith was struck by plague and resulting famine, which killed half the population in nine months, with 2,421 deaths in South Leith, 160 in Restalrig village, and 155 in Craigend or Calton village. Many of the dead were buried in Leith Links.

Until the mid-seventeenth century, the route to Leith from Edinburgh was either north, via the present-day Broughton Street to Canonmills and then along the western road to Leith (now Broughton Road and Bonnington Road), or from Holyrood by what is still called Easter Road. In 1650, when Oliver Cromwell's forces invaded Scotland, Sir Alexander Leslie, the commander of the Scottish army, had a defensive wall of earth built between Edinburgh and Leith, and this later became the broad road still known as Leith Walk.

At one time, according to the *Gazetteer*, a gibbet stood at Shrubhill, about halfway along Leith Walk, which was then a country road with market gardens and plant nurseries. Along it were second-hand bookstalls, 'shows' (funfair attractions) and shooting alleys.

5.2 Leith from 1800 onwards

It was not until 1800, that construction began of the first of what later became known as the Old Docks (the eastern wet dock), which was completed in 1806. The western dock was built between 1810 and 1817. (The Old Docks were filled in as part of the Leith Dock modernisation scheme in the late 1960s.)

Also in 1806, Leith Academy moved to the new building on Leith Links, which is still used by Leith Primary School, formerly Leith Academy Primary (see Chapter 15.2).

In 1833, North and South Leith were united as the municipal burgh of Leith. Five years later, Edinburgh's 500-year long domination of Leith ended when the right to receive customs duties on the cargoes of ships in Leith harbour was transferred from Edinburgh to Leith. At the same time, the Leith Dock Commission was set up to control the harbour and docks. To the north of the Old Docks, the Victoria Dock was opened in 1853. Land was reclaimed, allowing a long eastern breakwater to be built on the eastern side of the Water of Leith. Three new docks were constructed there: the Albert Dock opened in 1865, the Edinburgh Dock in 1881, and the Imperial Dock in 1904.

Besides shipping, Leith industries included: ship building, glass making, saw milling, flour milling, sugar refining, engineering, brewing, distilling, cement making, paint making, tanning and currying leather, rope-, twine- and sail-making, coopering (the manufacturing of buoys, as well as casks), lime juice making, and manufacturing chemicals.

During the First World War, Leith's industries made it the target of attacks by a Zeppelin airship (see Chapter 4.2). The port was also targeted by German aircraft in the Second World War (see Chapter 4.9).

Leith had resisted union with Edinburgh in 1896, when Portobello was assigned to the city, but in 1920, against the will of its people, the port was amalgamated with Edinburgh. The measure was taken despite a vote of 29,891 against and only 5,357 in favour in a plebiscite (or referendum) held earlier that year. At that time, Leith had a population of over 80,000. In *The Official Guide to Edinburgh*, which is undated but was apparently published shortly after the amalgamation, John Geddie writes:

> 'The burgh formed an enclave in Edinburgh territory with no other neighbour than the Firth. In the stranglehold of its bigger companion it had no freedom to expand and develop. On the other hand, Edinburgh needed Leith for its completion. Each, in fact, had need of the other.
>
> 'But obstacles, tangible and intangible, stood in the way of union – among others, sentiment, sometimes taking the form of prejudice – a difficult thing to grasp, and therefore to overcome.
>
> 'To the natural objection to merge the identity of their ancient burgh in the capital, there was added a traditional and inherited grudge against a neighbour who had once exercised authority over the harbour and community, and had not always done so wisely and justly.'

The volume of the 1966 *Third Statistical Account* on Edinburgh states that Leith was at that time the largest port on the east coast of Scotland and the second largest in Scotland.

Coal was Leith's biggest export during the 1930s, when almost 2,000,000 tons a year were shipped abroad, but by the mid-fifties, although still the biggest export, this figure had decreased to around 260,000 tons.

In 1964, the UK Government lent £6,000,000 to the Leith Dock Commission to finance a scheme to improve the docks and allow larger vessels to dock there in all tides. By 1969, a lock had been constructed at the mouth of the Western Harbour (at the end of the western breakwater, which was completed in 1942). The Leith Dock Commission became part of the Forth Ports Authority in 1967, and this became Forth Ports PLC in 1992. As well as Leith, Forth Ports owns five other ports in the Firth of Forth (Grangemouth, Rosyth, Burntisland, Kirkcaldy and Methil), plus Dundee and Tilbury.

Shipbuilding was carried on in Leith by the Henry Robb shipyard, which built around 500 ships and operated from 1918-1983. In 1924, the company took over the shipbuilders Hawthorns & Co (founded in 1881), then in 1926 purchased Cran & Somerville (founded in 1894), and in 1934, Ramage & Ferguson (founded in 1878).

Many of the Scottish Government's civil servants are employed at Victoria Quay, a new building constructed on redeveloped dockland between 1993 and 1996. In 1994, the former Leith Sailors' Home was refurbished to become the Malmaison Hotel. The Sailors' Home was built in 1883 to replace an earlier building constructed in 1840, and it was equipped with accommodation for 9 officers, 56 seamen and also provided space for 50 shipwrecked seamen in attic dormitories.

The former Royal Yacht *Britannia*, which went into service in 1954 and was decommissioned in 1997, is now based at Leith as a museum ship. *Britannia* is moored near the Ocean Terminal shopping centre, which was opened in 2001 on the site of the former Henry Robb shipyard.

A major ongoing regeneration plan for Edinburgh's waterfront (given outline approval by Edinburgh Council in 2011) envisages the redevelopment of the Leith Dock, Newhaven Harbour and Granton Harbour areas mainly for housing, although with some industrial and commercial use.

5.3 Newhaven

About a mile and a half east of the heart of North Leith lies the former village of Newhaven, which was founded in 1488 by King James III as 'Our Lady's Port of Grace', and became part of North Leith parish in 1631. The village was the king's 'new haven', as opposed to the 'old haven' of Blackness situated farther up the Firth of Forth, which was the port for the royal palace at Linlithgow.

In the sixteenth century, a ship named the *Michael* (usually known as the *Great Michael*) was built at Newhaven for James IV. At her launch in 1511, the *Great Michael* was the world's largest ship, at twice the size of her contemporary the English *Mary Rose*. According to popular legend, all the wood in Fife (except at Falkland Palace) was needed for her construction. In 1514, the *Great Michael* was sold to Louis XII of France at a bargain price after the Scots' defeat and the death of James IV at the Battle of Flodden the previous year.

Up to the mid-twentieth century, Newhaven was a thriving fishing village, with the men catching the fish and the women gutting them and carrying their 'creels' (large baskets) of fish to sell to Edinburgh housewives. Oysters were harvested in winter; cod, haddock and ling by line in summer; and herring using drift nets in late autumn.

According to the Newhaven-on-Forth website, www.newhaven onforth.org.uk, run by the Newhaven Action Group, the first fishermen to settle in Newhaven had come from Flanders to escape religious persecution, and many of Newhaven's old buildings reflect a Flemish style of architecture. The local fishing industry was run by the Society of Free Fishermen of Newhaven, founded in 1572. The society was originally set up as a charitable institution to help fisher families in times of trouble. From 1821, only the 'lawful sons of fishermen whose names were clear [i.e. not in debt] on the society books' were accepted as members. With the decline of Newhaven's fishing industry over the years and the provisions of the Welfare State, the members of the society voted for its dissolution in 1988.

By the nineteenth century, around 100 boats operated from Newhaven Harbour, crewed by about 400 fishermen. To handle the trade in fish, Edinburgh Council built a new Fishmarket next to the harbour in 1896. The fishing trade has now gone from Newhaven, the boats in its harbour are only used for leisure and pleasure, and many of the picturesque old houses have been replaced.

Chapter 6

EDINBURGH'S TOWNS AND VILLAGES

6.1 The growth of Edinburgh

Edinburgh has grown considerably since its beginnings on the Castle Rock at least 3,000 years ago. It was not until the mid-eighteenth century, however, that Edinburgh breached its traditional confines in the western part of the 'Royal Mile' (the road from the castle to Holyrood Palace) and overflowed into the surrounding parish of St Cuthbert's.

In 1766, houses were built in the newly laid out George Square just outside the southern part of the city, while from the following year Edinburgh began to exceed its boundaries to the north with the creation of the New Town.

From the twelfth century, the independent burgh of Canongate had grown up along the eastern section of the Royal Mile, with its own burgesses and freemen. The burgh's hammermen, tailors, wrights, baxters (bakers), shoemakers, weavers, fleshers (butchers) and barbers were incorporated by royal charter in 1630.

In 1856, through the Edinburgh Municipal Extension Act, the burgh of Canongate (including the large, detached portion consisting of Arthur's Seat and the surrounding hills in Holyrood Park) became part of Edinburgh, together with the former burghs of Calton (by the Calton Hill, just outside the city wall to the north-east) and Portsburgh (named after the West Port, the gateway to the south of Edinburgh Castle). Forty years later, the parish of Duddingston (including the seaside resort of Portobello) was also added to the city.

Leith had been made a burgh in 1833, but it was not amalgamated with Edinburgh until 1920. Also in 1920, the Midlothian parishes of Cramond, Corstorphine, Colinton and Liberton were incorporated into Edinburgh, which had been made a 'County of a City' in the nineteenth

*Midlothian parish map, c.1845. (Image from Statistical Accounts Online Service ©
University of Glasgow and University of Edinburgh. The Statistical Accounts of
Scotland are available online at http://edina.ac.uk/stat-acc-scot)*

century. During the twentieth century, and continuing into the twenty-
first, housing development has occurred in these formerly rural areas.

In 1975, Scotland's thirty-three counties were re-organised into nine
regions, plus three island areas (Orkney, Shetland and the Western
Isles). Most of the former counties of West Lothian and Midlothian, as
well as the whole county of East Lothian, were combined to form the
Lothian Region, which consisted of four districts: West Lothian,
Midlothian, East Lothian and the City of Edinburgh. As well as the
former County of the City of Edinburgh, the new City of Edinburgh
district included the parish of Dalmeny and the burgh of Queensferry
(both formerly in West Lothian), the parish of Kirkliston (previously
under the authorities of West Lothian and Midlothian), and the parishes
of Ratho and Currie (both in Midlothian).

In 1996, local government in Scotland was re-organised again, with
the twelve regions and island areas created by the 1975 changes

replaced by thirty-two unitary authorities. As a result of this second re-organisation, the four districts in the Lothian Region became unitary authorities within their existing boundaries.

As yet, Musselburgh, the coastal town that lies to the east of Edinburgh in the former parish of Inveresk, has not been absorbed by Edinburgh. In 1975, Musselburgh was transferred from Midlothian to East Lothian, in which it is the largest town, although Haddington, the former county town, remains the administrative centre.

6.2 St Cuthbert's parish

The once large parish of St Cuthbert's almost surrounded the Old Town of Edinburgh and the Canongate, and it had become part of the city by the late nineteenth century. The former villages of Water of Leith (now the Dean Village), the old Dean Village (now demolished) and Stockbridge were situated in the north of St Cuthbert's parish, and the village of Morningside in the south.

Old mansions in the parish included:

- **Grange House**, the estate of which was originally the Grange or granary of St Giles' Church as early as the twelfth century. Grange House became the home of the Dick family in 1679, and later of the Dick Lauders, when Isabel, the Dick heiress, married Sir Andrew Lauder of Fountainhall in 1731. In the 1840s, large stone houses were built on the Grange estate, which is now a conservation area, and Grange House was demolished in 1936.
- **Bruntsfield House** also belonged to a branch of the Lauder family from 1381 until it was sold to George Warrender of Lochend in 1695. The house is now part of James Gillespie's School (see Chapter 15.6).
- The original **Whitehouse** was built around 1505 in what is now Whitehouse Loan, and later in the sixteenth century it was held by James Hepburn, Earl of Bothwell, the third husband of Mary, Queen of Scots. The house and estate then passed to Euphemia, Lady Cliftonhall, who was found guilty of witchcraft and burnt on Castle Hill in June 1591. The present building was constructed about 1670, and there, in 1834, the Roman Catholic Bishop James Gillis founded St Margaret's Convent, the first post-Reformation convent in Scotland. From 1986-1993, the building was a seminary called Gillis College and it is now the Gillis Centre, a Catholic conference centre.

- **Merchiston Castle** (see Chapters 15.11 and 16.3) belonged to the Napier family from at least 1438, at which time it was known as the King's House. The castle was bombarded by both the King's and Queen's parties during the civil war in 1572.
- The original **Craig House** on Easter Craiglockhart Hill dated from the mid-fourteenth century, but was destroyed by the Earl of Hertford's troops in 1544, during King Henry VIII of England's 'Rough Wooing' of Mary, Queen of Scots, whom he sought as a bride for his son, the future Edward VI. A new Craig House was built in 1565, and in the nineteenth century was the home of the historian John Hill Burton, whose extensive library took up half of the house. Later in the century it became Craig House Hospital, a psychiatric hospital, and after refurbishment, the Craighouse Campus of Napier University (see Chapter 16.3).
- **East Coates House** was built by the Byres family in the early seventeenth century and restored in 1830 by Sir Patrick Walker. His unmarried daughters, Barbara and Mary, left their entire fortune, including the house, to the Scottish Episcopal Church on condition that a cathedral would be built with the money. East Coates House has therefore stood since 1873 in the grounds of St Mary's Cathedral and it was the home of the Cathedral Choir School (St Mary's Music School from 1971) until 1995, when the house became the Scottish Episcopal Church's Theological Institute.
- Standing to the south-west of Holyrood Park, **Salisbury Green** was built around 1780, and its neighbour **St Leonard's Hall** about ninety years later. The latter house was constructed in the older Scottish baronial style (with 'pepper-pot' turrets), while the former had already been remodelled in the same style in the 1860s. St Leonard's Hall was built for Thomas Nelson Junior, while Salisbury Green was the home of his brother William (the sons of Thomas Nelson of the Edinburgh publishing company Thomas Nelson and Sons). Both houses were used as halls of residence by Edinburgh University in the second half of the twentieth century, although St Leonard's Hall is now an administrative centre for the University's Pollock Halls (of residence) site, while Salisbury Green is operated as a hotel by the University.

6.3 The parish of Cramond
Cramond parish was situated to the north-west of Edinburgh on the

Firth of Forth, east of the parish of Dalmeny in West Lothian, west of St Cuthbert's and north of Corstorphine. Now a suburban area, the parish remained a rural area, consisting of two villages and a few large houses with their surrounding estates, up to the mid-twentieth century. A small part of the parish lay in West Lothian until 1891, when it was transferred to Dalmeny.

Cramond's name is a corruption of 'Caer Aman', meaning 'the fort on the stream', in this case the Almond, a small river which runs into the Firth of Forth. The fort was built by the Romans in 142 AD, during their second incursion into what is now Scotland (see Chapter 1.4). A harbour was constructed at the mouth of the river by the fort's garrison of nearly 500 troops. Although the very name of Cramond advertises the existence of a fort, the remains of the site were not discovered until 1954. You can see the various items that have since been unearthed – including the 'Cramond Lioness', discovered in 1997 – at Edinburgh's National Museum of Scotland (see Appendix A 4.1).

A medieval parish church existed in Cramond but it was replaced by a new building in 1656, incorporating the earlier church's fifteenth-century tower, which received a castellated parapet in 1811. Seventeenth-century services could last up to three or four hours, including an hour-long Bible reading and a two-hour sermon, and could be disturbed – or perhaps enlivened – by parishioners' dogs fighting in the church.

The church also saw occasions with more levity. The Reverend Robert Walker, minister of Cramond Kirk from 1776-1784, was portrayed by the artist Sir Henry Raeburn as the 'skating minister' in a painting from the 1790s, which shows the Revd. Walker skating on a frozen Duddingston Loch.

Among Cramond Churchyard's memorials are many dedicated to the 'heritors' (local landowners), including the Howison (later Howison-Craufurd) family. In the sixteenth century, Jock Howison is said to have saved King James V from a gang of ruffians at Old Cramond Brig, when the King was travelling alone and incognito, as he was fond of doing. As a reward, the King granted Jock his land at Braehead in perpetuity, with the proviso that he and his descendants must always provide the monarch with a basin of water and a napkin, should he or she pass by. Sir Walter Scott arranged for this to be done when King George IV was on his way from Holyrood to Hopetoun House in 1822.

Cramond Tower may have been part of the palace of the Bishop of Dunkeld, who held Cramond for King David I in the twelfth century. The tower was certainly occupied by various owners from the fourteenth century up to 1622, when it was purchased by the Inglis family. In 1680, however, John Inglis built the nearby Cramond House, which the Inglis family then moved to. The tower was left unoccupied and became ruinous over the following 300 years. In 1978, Cramond Tower was bought by Eric Jamieson, who restored the building. Mr Jamieson's son George, a professional taxidermist, now lives in the tower, the ground floor of which is used as a gallery for paintings and taxidermy displays.

Cramond House was extended in the late eighteenth and early nineteenth century, when Lady Torphichen, the daughter of Sir John Inglis, added a new front elevation to the house. Cramond House then passed to the Craigie-Halkett family, who lived there until the last of the line died in 1959, in reduced circumstances. The house was bought by the Church of Scotland in 1971.

There were once five, now mostly ruined, mills along the River Almond between Old Cramond Brig and the Firth of Forth: Dowie's, Peggie's, Craigie's, Fairafar and Cockle Mills. The mills were originally used for milling grain, but in the eighteenth century, they became the basis of the introduction of the Industrial Revolution to Cramond. The oldest of the mills was Cockle Mill, which belonged to the Bishops of Dunkeld in 1179, and is now used as a private house. The Smith and Wright Company of Leith (founded in 1747) bought the Cockle and Fairafar Mills in 1752, converted the Cockle Mill to iron rolling and slitting, and used the site to produce iron hoops for barrels, carts and barrows.

The Fairafar Mill was not used for iron working until 1759, however. In that year, the Carron Company of Falkirk bought the two mills, but sold them in 1770 to the William Cadells, senior and junior, who founded the Cramond Iron Company. Peggie's and Dowie's Mills were also bought by the Cadells, in 1781 and 1782 respectively, and at both sites the company made spades, hoes, chains and anchors and also employed a colony of nail makers. In 1807, the output of Peggie's Mill was switched to making coarse cartridge paper.

The Cadells were successful up to around 1797, but the Cramond iron works had lost its former importance by 1810. Steam power had been introduced by 1852, but the Cadells sold their Cramond business in 1865. After this Peggie's Mill was used by John MacKay in his manufacturing chemist business and Dowie's Mill was used as a sawmill. Furniture was produced at both mills from 1923-1934.

The Craigie Mill was the only one of the Cramond Iron Company mills situated on the former West Lothian bank of the river, and it was used as a grain and waulk mill for washing, stretching and beating woven yarn. The mill went into decline in the late eighteenth century.

As well as Cramond Village (much of which was demolished in the nineteenth century so that Lady Torphichen could extend the Cramond House estate), the parish of Cramond also included the village of Davidson's Mains (known up to about 1850 as Muttonhole, the name being possibly derived from 'Moot Hill', a place of judgement) at the junction of Queensferry Road from Edinburgh and Ferry Road from Leith.

It was not until 1823 that Queensferry Road (named Hillhouse Road at this point) was realigned to run to the south of the village, rather than through it, (as what is now called Corbiehill Road does). The new name for 'Muttonhole' came from the Davidson family, who owned the Muirhouse estate north of the village. A member of this family became Archbishop of Canterbury in 1903.

Major houses in the vicinity included: Lauriston Castle (see Appendix A6.3); (New) Barnton House (formerly known as Cramond Regis or King's Cramond, and demolished about 1920), most of the estate of which now forms the golf courses of the Royal Burgess Golfing Society and the Bruntsfield Links Golfing Society; Marchfield (at one time the home of Sir Andrew Murray, Lord Provost of Edinburgh from 1947-1951); and Craigcrook Castle (shown as Craig Rook on old maps).

The sixteenth-century castle was, in the early 1800s, the home of the publisher Archibald Constable. The next tenant was the lawyer Francis Jeffrey, who was born in Edinburgh in 1773 and lived at Craigcrook from 1815 until his death in 1850. Jeffrey became the co-founder in 1802 of the *Edinburgh Review* (which he edited for nearly twenty-six years from 1803), he was twice elected Rector of the University of Glasgow (in 1820 and 1822), was made Lord Advocate in 1830, elected to Parliament in 1831, and became a Lord of the Court of Session in 1834.

After being occupied by a number of private tenants, the castle was bought in 1968 by an architectural practice, which completely refurbished the building. It continued in commercial use until it was offered for sale as a private residence in May 2014, at a price of £6,000,000, making it Scotland's most expensive private home!

6.4 The parish of Corstorphine

The name Corstorphine (or 'Crostorfin', as it was spelt in 1128), according to William J Watson's *Celtic Place-names of Scotland*, means 'Torfin's crossing [over the hill]'; Torfin is a personal name.

Like Cramond, Corstorphine remained rural until the early twentieth century, when the large scale house-building began, turning the area into the Edinburgh suburb that it is today. Before Corstorphine was incorporated into Edinburgh in 1920, the parish was bounded on the north by Cramond, on the east by St Cuthbert's parish, on the south by Ratho, Currie and Colinton parishes, and on the west by part of Kirkliston parish which lay in the county of Midlothian.

According to the Reverend David Horne, in the *New Statistical Account of Scotland* (see Chapter 17), the parish of Corstorphine included within its boundaries part of the ancient parish of Gogar. It also encompassed Ravelston and Saughton, which had been detached from St Cuthbert's parish by the Teind (Tithe) Commission of 1627, and added to Corstorphine in 1633.

Corstorphine comprised two villages: the original 'low' village in Corstorphine High Street, and the newer 'high' village in St John's Road (the main road leading to Glasgow, now the A8). The low village grew up between two lochs which had been completely drained by 1837: Gogar Loch (to the west of the village) and Corstorphine Loch (to the east). The two lochs and the small area between them stretched about 5 miles from east to west.

Near the low village, there was a mineral spring the water of which was thought to cure scrofula. Writing in 1839, the Revd. Horne states that:

> 'For many years previous to the end of the last century, and at the commencement of the present, this well was in great repute, and for the sake of it, Corstorphine was much resorted to as a watering-place, so much so, that in the month of May 1749, a stage-chaise was set up, which travelled between Corstorphine and Edinburgh eight or nine times every week-day, and four times on Sunday.

'It is said that one of the ladies of the family of Dick of Prestonfield and Corstorphine experienced so much benefit from using the water, that she took up her residence in the village, and erected a building over the well, placing a pump on it so as to make it more convenient and accessible to the inhabitants. This erection was allowed to fall into disrepair, when the well lost its popularity, and the last vestige of it was removed about fourteen years ago.'

The principal family in the parish were the Forresters, owners of the Corstorphine estate from 1376-1698. The founder of the line, Adam Forrester, an Edinburgh merchant, was Provost of Edinburgh in 1373, Sheriff of Lothian in 1383 and Keeper of the Great Seal in 1390. He was captured at the Battle of Hamildon Hill in 1402 and presented to King Henry IV of England in Parliament, where he acted as spokesman for the other prisoners.

A later Forrester, Sir Alexander, led pilgrimages to the shrine of Saint Thomas à Beckett in Canterbury in 1464 and to that of John de Amyace in the north of France two years later. George, the tenth head of the family was made Lord Forrester of Corstorphine in 1633, but he proved to be the last of the male line.

After the Battle of Dunbar in 1650, the Corstorphine area was occupied for a year by the victorious English troops of Oliver Cromwell. Because Lord Forrester was trying to rouse the country against the English, the soldiers defaced figures of the Forresters in the parish church, damaged the church and laid waste the Corstorphine estate.

On the death of the first Lord Forrester in 1651, the estate and the title were entailed on James Baillie, the husband of Lord Forrester's fourth daughter, Joanna. On 26 August 1679, James Baillie was run through with his own sword by Joanna's niece, Christian Nimmo (née Hamilton), his former mistress, whom he had slandered. The deed took place at the ancient sycamore tree that stood in the village until it was blown down on Boxing Day in 1998. Christian was beheaded in Edinburgh on 12 November 1679 and her ghost was said to haunt the sycamore tree.

On the death of the second Lord Forrester, his brother and heir, William Baillie, did not take the title because of the scandal, and he died eighteen months later. Instead, William's son became the fourth Lord

Forrester in 1684. The estate was encumbered by debts, however, and was sold to Hugh Wallace of Ingliston, a solicitor, in 1698. Sir James Dick of Prestonfield bought the Corstorphine estate in 1713, and it remained in his family for 150 years.

The home of the Forresters and their successors was Corstorphine Castle, of which nothing now remains. The castle was built in the fourteenth century, south of the low village, in what is now Castle Avenue. When Corstorphine Castle was demolished around 1790, the workmen discovered a hoard of gold and silver coins. According to the *New Statistical Account*, Oatman Barclay, the overseer, gave some of the coins to the other workmen and kept the rest for himself, enabling him to give up work and live off the proceeds for the rest of his life.

The original parish church in Corstorphine, St Mary's, was mentioned in a charter of King David I in 1128. In 1404, Adam Forrester built a small chapel next to St Mary's for use as a burial place for the Forrester family and dedicated it to St John the Baptist. His son, Sir John Forrester, extended the chapel and converted it into a church with a distinctive square tower around 1429. The neighbouring St Mary's was demolished in 1646, some of the material from it being used in further extensions of St John the Baptist's Church.

Other estates in the parish of Corstorphine were Gogar, Clermiston, East Craigs, Ravelston and Saughton. In the late eighteenth century, part of the Clermiston estate was leased to the father of Sir Walter Scott.

According to the *New Statistical Account*, the village of Gogar at one time had three hundred inhabitants, but by 1838, the number had decreased to just twenty-four. Other villages in the parish of Corstorphine at that time were Stanhope-Mills (named after Janet Stanhope, the wife of Richard Watson of Saughton, who lived around 1550) in Saughton with a population of sixty-seven, and Four-mile-hill with forty-nine.

In 1909, the Royal Zoological Society of Scotland was founded as a non-profit organisation devoted to the study and conservation of wildlife. Edinburgh's zoo was opened in July 1913 on the slopes of Corstorphine Hill, with the addition of an aquarium in July 1927. In 1902, a railway line began running to a station near the old village and, until the station closed in 1967, a suburban train service operated over the line to the Waverley Station and beyond. Bus services followed in 1906, and a tramway service from 1923-1954.

6.5 The parish of Colinton

According to Stuart Harris's *The Place Names of Edinburgh*, Colinton was 'Colgyntoun' in 1296 (meaning the farm of someone named Colgan). The name later became 'Collington', a form used up to the end of the eighteenth century, although a version without the 'g' was also used as early as 1438.

Colinton is situated to the south of Corstorphine and St Cuthbert's parishes, to the west of Liberton, to the east of Currie, and to the north of the parishes of Penicuik, Glencorse and Lasswade (which are still within Midlothian). The Water of Leith, which rises in the Pentland Hills, flows through the parish.

Colinton Parish Church (dedicated to St Cuthbert and known as 'Halis' or Hailes Church prior to 1700) was founded around 1095 by Ethelred, the third son of King Malcolm III and Queen Margaret, although there seems to have been an earlier church on the same site. The present church dates from 1771, with improvements carried out in 1837 and 1908.

Hailes, which means 'the land between the waters', (i.e. the Water of Leith and the Murray Burn) had once been a large estate. It was divided by the fifteenth century into Over or Easter Hailes (which became the Redhall estate, including Colinton, Redhall, Oxgangs, Comiston, Swanston, Dreghorn, Bonaly and Woodhall), Nether or Wester Hailes, and the Kirklands of Hailes (or Spylaw).

Robert Louis Stevenson's maternal grandfather, the Reverend Lewis Balfour, was minister of Colinton from 1823-1860. In 1839, Balfour wrote the article about the parish in the *New Statistical Account* (see Chapter 17). In it, he writes that the Foulis family is the most ancient in the parish, and they are thought to have come to Scotland from France in the reign of Malcolm III, acquiring the lands of Colinton in 1519.

James Foulis of Colinton was one of the commissioners appointed in August 1543 (after the Treaty of Edinburgh that July) to negotiate

Robert Louis Stevenson (1850-1894). From Francis Watt's Book of Edinburgh Anecdote *(T N Foulis, 1912).*

the marriage of the eight-month-old Mary, Queen of Scots and the six-year old future King Edward VI of England. Unfortunately, the negotiations failed and the Scottish Parliament did not ratify the treaty.

In the following century, Alexander Foulis of Colinton was created a baronet in 1634. His son, Sir James Foulis, became a Senator of the Scottish College of Justice under the title of Lord Colinton. Sir Alexander's grandson, Sir James Foulis, was also a judge under the title of Lord Redford (as his father was still living at the time) and he was a member of the last of the old Scottish Parliaments and the first British Parliament.

Although the Colinton estate was transferred into other hands, the baronetcy passed to the cadet family of Foulis of Woodhall, also in the parish. The Reverend Balfour adds, as a note, that:

'This family seems at one time to have possessed nearly the whole of the parish of Hailes. [In] 1609, James Foulis de Collingtoune was ratified in the lands of Collingtoune, Swanston, Dreghorn, Boneyley, Baddis, Pitmure Oxgangs, Comiston, Reidhall. [In] 1641, Sir Alexander Foulis is ratified in Collingtoun Oxgangs, the vicarage of Hailes, in the teinds [tithes] of town and lands of Craiglockhart Oxgangs, portions of Boneley, Dreghorn, and Swanston.

'[In] 1661, July 12, anent [regarding] Lord Collingtoune's losses, inter alia, in 1650, his whole tenement, tennant houses, barnes, byres, and haill [whole] onsets, in the town and lands of New Mains, Craiglockhart, and Benbridge, burned by the Usurper's [Cromwell's] army, £4,000 Scots. The whole of his plenishing [furnishings] within the manor place of Collingtoun, burnt or taken away, all the doors and windows, iron work, and much of the loft and roof were burned, pulled down, destroyed, or taken away, by the said Usurpers, and that he had several other houses destroyed, and much of his planting cut, all estimated to £10,000 Scots, his corns destroyed, estimated at £3,083 Scots.'

In 1839, the landowners in the parish of Colinton were **Alexander Trotter of Dreghorn**; Sir Thomas Gibson Carmichael of Hailes, Bart;

Richard Trotter of (Mortonhall) Swanston; **Sir James Forrest of Comiston, Bart; John Inglis of Redhall; Sir James Foulis of Woodhall**, Bart.; Gillespie's Hospital (see Chapter 15.6); **Dr Alexander Monro of Craiglockhart**, Professor of Anatomy in the University of Edinburgh; Sir John S Forbes of Pitsligo and Fettercairn, Bart of Colinton House; J Home Rigg of Colinton Mains; and Andrew Grieve, Writer to the Signet, of Hole Mill. (NB: The names in bold type are those of landowners who lived in the parish, at least during the summer, if not all year round.)

The Reverend Balfour mentions that Edinburgh families often lived in the parish during the summer, as a rural retreat from the city. He adds that around 1832 Dr W P Alison, Professor of the Theory of Medicine at Edinburgh University, took the remainder of a long lease of Woodville ('a small but pretty property') with his father, the late Reverend Archibald Alison of St Paul's Chapel, Edinburgh. In addition, Alexander Clapperton, an Edinburgh merchant, and his family spent each summer at a small farm called Spylaw Bank, which he had leased from Gillespie's Hospital.

Large houses in the parish were:

- **Colinton Castle**, built in the fifteenth or sixteenth century for the Foulis family, and a ruin since the early nineteenth century;
- **Craiglockhart Castle**, a small fifteenth-century ruined tower house, was built either by the Lockharts of Lee or the Kincaid family, and is now part of the Craiglockhart Campus of Edinburgh Napier University (see Chapter 16.3);
- **Dreghorn Castle**, originally built in the seventeenth century for Sir William Murray (Master of Works to King Charles II), rebuilt about 1820 and demolished in 1955;
- **Woodhall House**, built around 1630 for Adam Cunninghame, Lord Woodhall, whose family owned the house until it was sold to the Foulis family in the early eighteenth century;
- **Redford House**, which dates from the mid-seventeenth century and to which was added, in 1884, some of the ornamental stonework from the original Edinburgh Royal Infirmary (designed by William Adam and built in 1738) by the then owner, Robert Andrew Macfie of Dreghorn;
- **Redhall House**, designed by James Robertson and built in 1758 for

George Inglis of Auchendinny, was sold to Edinburgh Corporation at the end of the Second World War, used as a children's home and then council offices, and is now standing empty;

- **Colinton House**, built for Sir William Forbes between 1801 and 1806, and now part of Merchiston Castle School (see Chapter 15.11);
- **Comiston House**, built in 1815 for Sir James Forrest;
- **Craiglockhart House** was built in 1823 for Dr Alexander Monro of Edinburgh University;
- **Craiglockhart Hydropathic** was built on the Craiglockhart estate between 1877 and 1880, and was first used as a hotel, then a convent and Craiglockhart College of Education (now part of Edinburgh Napier University – see Chapter 16.3). During the First World War, the building was converted into the Craiglockhart War Hospital for Officers, where Dr William Halse Rivers treated men suffering from shell shock, including the 'war poets' Siegfried Sassoon and Wilfred Owen.

Besides Colinton itself, other villages within the parish of Colinton were Juniper Green (the site of a number of mills on the Water of Leith), Longstone & Slateford (also the site of mills, as well as a bleachfield, quarries, cattle markets and slaughterhouses), and Swanston (still a village today, and the location of Swanston Cottage, the summer home of the family of Robert Louis Stevenson).

In August 1874, a railway line from Edinburgh was opened to Balerno (in the parish of Currie), with stations at Colinton, Juniper Green and Currie. Passengers services ceased in October 1943, but goods trains continued to run on the line until the early 1960s.

Between 1909 and 1915, Redford Barracks was built in the area between Colinton Road and Colinton Mains Drive, to house both infantry and cavalry, and in 1923, it became home to the British Army garrison formerly in Edinburgh Castle.

6.6 The parish of Liberton

Liberton was a large parish, lying to the south-east of St Cuthbert's parish, south of Canongate and Duddingston, east of Colinton, west of Inveresk and Newton, and north of Lasswade. As well as the settlements of Kirk Liberton, Over Liberton, Nether Liberton and Liberton Dams, the parish included the villages of Burdiehouse,

Gilmerton and Straiton. Liberton's north-eastern area was, at one time, the ancient parish of Niddrie, which included the village of the same name, as well as the old and new villages of Newcraighall.

The parish's name was traditionally thought to originate from 'Lepertown', a leper colony. In his book *The Place Names of Edinburgh*, however, Stuart Harris derives the name Liberton from the Anglian 'hlida beretun', in which 'bere' means barley, 'tun' farm and 'hlid' is a slope.

The Reverend James Begg, writing in the New Statistical Account in 1839, listed the main landowners in the parish as Walter Little Gilmour of Liberton and Craigmillar; **Richard Trotter of Mortonhall and Charterhall**; Andrew Wauchope of Niddry-Marshal; Sir David Baird of Newbyth; **David Anderson of Moredun**; the Marquis of Abercorn; **Sir William Rae of St Catherine's**; Miss Innes of Drum; Miss Sivright of Meggetland; James Johnston of Straiton; Sir Robert Dick of Prestonfield; Lord Melville; Wardlaw Ramsay of Whitehill; Mrs Gilchrist of Sunnyside; John Wauchope of Edmonstone; John Tod of Todhills; Robert Bruce of Kennet; and William Tullis of Mount Vernon. (NB: Landowners who lived in the parish, at least some of the time, are shown in bold type. Mrs Gilmour of Craigmillar was also resident.)

Large houses in the parish of Liberton included:

- **Craigmillar Castle** (see Appendix 6.4).
- There has been a house on or near the present **Drum House** for at least 600 years, according to Malcom Cant's *Villages of Edinburgh*. For most of this time, the Drum estate was owned by the Somerville family. The present house was built for the Somervilles by William Adam between 1726 and 1734, incorporating part of the previous house erected by John Mylne in 1584.
- **Moredun House** (originally known as Goodtrees or Gutters) was constructed in the fifteenth century and was owned by the Herries, Somerville, McCulloch, Stewart (from 1648-1775), Moncrieff, Anderson and Welsh families. It was David Stewart Moncrieff who renamed the house 'Moredun', after a hill on the Moncrieff estate in Perthshire. In 1923, the house was bought with the intention of turning it into a convalescent home for wounded servicemen, but the building was in too poor a state of repair for renovation and instead it was demolished. The Murray Home, now owned by the Scottish

Veterans Housing Association, was built on the site in 1929. In 1924, part of the Moredun estate was bought by the Animal Diseases Research Association as the site for the Moredun Research Institute, which was opened in 1927.

- **Liberton Tower** in Over Liberton was built in the late fifteenth century, and was owned by the Dalmahoys, the Forresters of Corstorphine, and then the Littles, who had **Liberton House** constructed nearby in the late sixteenth century. After agricultural use since 1610, Liberton Tower is now on a long lease to Castles of Scotland Preservation Trust and is hired out for self-catering holidays. Liberton House was owned by the Littles up to the mid-twentieth century, and then until 2010 by a firm of architects who restored it after a fire in 1991.

- **Gilmerton House**, or the **Place of Gilmerton**, was probably built in the mid-sixteenth century, and has been owned by several families over the years, including the Kinlochs and the Beards of Newbyth. By the end of the nineteenth century, the house had been sub-divided and rented out to miners. Gilmerton House later became derelict and was demolished in the 1970s.

- **Inch House** dates back to at least 1617, when the owners were the Winram family. In 1660, the Gilmours of Craigmillar purchased the property but did not live in it until the late eighteenth century. In 1945, the Gilmours sold the house to the Edinburgh Corporation and it is now a community centre.

- **Niddry** or **Niddrie House** (also known as **Niddrie Marischal House**) was built by the Wauchope family about 1636, on the site of a former medieval tower. The Wauchopes owned the land from the early fifteenth to the twentieth century. The house was semi-derelict by 1953 and demolished about 1968.

- In 1980, the architects responsible for renovating Liberton House also restored **Peffermill House**, which was originally built in 1636. The house became a farmhouse, and was later divided into several flats, then restored as a single dwelling by 1920. There is an interesting story linked to the house. In September 1724, 22-year-old Margaret Dickson was hanged in the Grassmarket for concealing her pregnancy, when her child died a few days after it was born. Her body was put in a coffin on a cart bound for Musselburgh. She revived, however, outside the Ram's Heid Inn, within the grounds of

Peffermill House. As she was now legally regarded as dead, she could not be hanged again and lived for another forty years, known as 'Half-hangit Maggie Dickson'.

- **Brunstane House** was erected by John Maitland, 1st Duke of Lauderdale in 1639, incorporating parts of earlier houses on the site, dating from the fourteenth and sixteenth centuries and once owned by the Crichton family. Since then the house has had many owners.
- **Southfield House** was converted into private flats in 2001, having been used as a sanatorium by the Royal Victoria Hospital from 1902. The house, which dates back to the seventeenth century, was rebuilt in 1875 for the coach-builder John Croall, who had bought the Southfield estate in 1849. Earlier owners included the banker Sir William Forbes at the end of the eighteenth century.
- **Mortonhall** was completed in 1769 for Thomas Trotter, 9th Baron Mortonhall, whose family had been proprietors of the Mortonhall estate since 1635. The estate had been granted to Henry Sinclair of Roslin by King Robert the Bruce in 1317, and a fortified house had been built on what would become the site of the eighteenth century house. Many of the estate's farms have become housing estates, golf clubs and the Mortonhall Crematorium. Mortonhall House has been converted into offices and flats.
- **Sunnyside House** was built by the architect Robert Adam around 1780, and its name changed to Kingston Grange about 1850. It is now the club house of Liberton Golf Club, which was established in the 1920s.
- **St Katherine's House** was built in 1806, and later became a children's home, and then a centre for the elderly. It is now a restaurant called the Balmwell, named after the neighbouring St Katherine's Balm Well. The well, containing water and an oily substance from the shale deposits beneath, was visited by King James IV in 1504, and a building was constructed around it on the orders of James VI in 1617.

The Reverend Begg reported that, in 1839, there were thirty-two shops selling spirits in the parish of Liberton, which he felt was 'just thirty too many'. No ale-houses were allowed to exist, however, on the Niddrie, Mortonhall, Moredun or Brunstane estates.

Commenting on the housing in the parish, the Reverend Begg surmised that little had been done to improve the cottages in which most people lived. Of the parish's population of nearly 4,000, only 207 were judged above the 'poor and working classes', and this number included teachers, farmers, publicans and shopkeepers. Some of the houses occupied by the rest of the local people were 'very wretched'.

The Gilmerton Junior Friendly Society was established in 1787 by the village's carters to provide sickness and funeral benefits to its members, and continued to do so until the advent of the Welfare State in the mid-twentieth century. The society held an annual 'Play Day' on the last Friday in July, but not everyone approved of this custom. The Reverend Begg wrote in the *New Statistical Account*:

'The only peculiar games here are what are called 'carter's plays'. The carters have friendly societies for the purpose of supporting each other in old age or during ill-health, and with the view partly of securing a day's recreation, and partly of recruiting their numbers and funds, they have an annual procession.

'Every man decorates his carthorse with flowers and ribbons, and a regular procession is made, accompanied by a band of music, through this and some of the neighbouring parishes. To crown [it] all, there is an uncouth uproarious race with carthorses on the public road, which draws forth a crowd of Edinburgh idlers, and [it] all ends in a dinner, for which a fixed sum is paid. Much rioting and profligacy often take place in connection with these amusements, and the whole scene is melancholy.

'There are other societies in the parish which have also annual parades with a similar result. These societies have undoubtedly been in some respects useful, but the 'plays' are fortunately rapidly declining; and it is to be hoped that savings banks, in which there is neither risk nor temptation to drunkenness, will soon become the universal depositories for the surplus earnings of the people.'

In 1839, the parish of Liberton was still very much a rural area, with thirty-four farms. According to the Reverend Begg, the farms varied in size from 40-268 acres, with the majority being over 100 acres, and six farms consisting of more than 200 acres. Some tenants rented two or more farms, which resulted in combined areas of more than 300 acres.

Edinburgh is not usually thought of as an industrial area, and although Liberton was primarily an agricultural parish, coal-mining was carried on in the villages of Gilmerton, Niddrie and Newcraighall. In Gilmerton and Niddrie, coal mines were in operation for hundreds of years.

In May 1884, a fire in one of the Niddrie pits caused the deaths of the following seven people: William Hamilton (aged fifty-one, who left a wife and ten children), George Hill (fifteen), David Kerr (seventeen), John Middleton (sixteen), Neil Paton (twenty-two, from Dunfermline), Michael Scanlon (fourteen) and David Smith (twenty-five, who had fought in Egypt with the 78th Highlanders). Ten men (or, in some cases, boys) were also found unconscious, but survived, including William Hamilton (sixteen), the son of the William Hamilton among the dead.

Limestone had been obtained in Gilmerton 'from time immemorial', according to the Reverend Begg, at first using open-cast methods, and later through underground mining. A different seam of limestone was worked at Burdiehouse and Straiton from about 1750, using open-cast mining and, from around 1800, by deep mining. The limestone was sold to builders in Edinburgh by men who would take homing pigeons with them, so they could send a bird home carrying details of the order for delivery that same day.

Shale was also mined at Straiton during the nineteenth century for the production of shale oil. Liberton's mining days are all in the past, however: no coal, limestone or shale is mined in the parish today.

An oddity in Gilmerton is an underground 'cove', or cave, cut into the sandstone about 10 feet below the surface, situated near the corner of Drum Street (the main A7 road) and Newtoft Street. In 1792, Gilmerton Cove was described by the Reverend Thomas Whyte, in an article published in the *Transactions of the Society of Antiquaries of Scotland*, as having been constructed between 1719 and 1724 by a blacksmith named George Paterson, who was the owner of the land. Paterson, along with his wife and family, lived and worked in several rooms in the cove until his death in 1735.

In *Villages of Edinburgh, Volume 2*, Malcolm Cant describes the cove as having a main passageway about 40 feet long, with several rooms branching off it on either side. On one side is a forge and another room measuring about 14ft by 7ft. On the other side are several other rooms and the beginnings of a tunnel.

In 1897, F R Coles, Assistant Keeper of the National Museum of Antiquities (now the National Museum of Scotland), visited the cove with J Balfour Paul, Lord Lyon King of Arms, and George Good, FSA, who had lived in Liberton all his life. The men carried out a three-day survey and concluded that the cove was about a century older than the Reverend Whyte had previously thought, and that it could not have been the work of only one man. Their view was that George Paterson had merely lived and worked in the cove, rather than constructed it himself.

The cove has since been restored by Gilmerton Heritage Trust and Edinburgh Council, and has been open to the public since 2003.

6.7 The parish of Duddingston (including Portobello)

Duddingston was a wedge-shaped parish stretching from the detached part of the parish of Canongate (now Holyrood Park) in the west to the Firth of Forth and Inveresk parish in the east. In the north-west, Duddingston was bounded by South Leith and in the south by the Niddrie area of the parish of Liberton.

Duddingston parish was known as Treverlen, or Traverlen, before the mid-thirteenth century, according to Stuart Harris's *The Place Names of Edinburgh*. Harris derives that name from the British 'tre war lyn' ('farm on the loch'), and suggests that it may have referred to a crannog or lake dwelling said to have been situated on Duddingston Loch (which was more than twice as large before 1750 than it is today). In 1778, some late Bronze Age spears and javelins were found in the loch, dating back to around 800 BC.

The name Duddingston comes from 'Dodinestoun' ('Dodin's farm'). Dodin was the Anglo-Norman to whom the estate was feued in the mid-twelfth century by the monks of Kelso Abbey, who had received it about 1130, probably from King David I.

In 1630, the Reverend Robert Monteith, the son of a fisherman, became the minister of Duddingston's twelfth-century Norman church. He is said to have unwisely entered into a liaison with the married Lady Hamilton of Priestfield and was defrocked when this was discovered. Monteith then fled to Paris, joined the Roman Catholic Church, and sought favour from Cardinal Richelieu. On being asked by the Cardinal from which branch of the family he was descended, Monteith replied 'Salmonet'. This was accepted by Richelieu, and Monteith went on to have a successful life in the Catholic Church, being later installed as a canon of Notre Dame Cathedral, and devoting much of his time to historical research.

On the east side of Duddingston Loch lies (Wester) Duddingston Village, which is relatively secluded and has retained its rural village character. The Sheep Heid Inn claims to be Edinburgh's oldest pub, dating from around 1360, and to have entertained Mary, Queen of Scots, King James VI and 'Bonnie Prince Charlie'.

In 1674, the estate of Duddingston passed from the Dukes of Lauderdale to the 1st Duke of Argyll, through his marriage to Lord Lauderdale's daughter. Then, in 1745, the estate was bought by James Hamilton, the 8th Earl of Abercorn, who in 1760, commissioned Sir William Chambers to design Duddingston House, where many Scottish politicians visited.

In 1894, Duddingston Golf Club was opened within the grounds, as was Holyrood High School in the 1960s. During the Second World War, a prisoner of war camp was constructed in the grounds. Duddingston House became the Mansion House Hotel in 1963, but in the 1990s, it was restored and used as offices for the Burrell Company, a firm of architects.

At Nairne Lodge (originally called Caroline Cottage) lived Carolina, Lady Nairne (née Oliphant), who had moved there in 1806, on her marriage to her cousin Major William Nairne at the age of forty, after a twenty-three-year engagement. Lady Nairne wrote many poems and Jacobite songs, such as 'Will ye no come back again?', 'Charlie is my darling' and 'Wi' a hundred pipers an' a' an' a''. Nairne Lodge is now the Lady Nairne Grill and Premier Inn Edinburgh East.

Prestonfield House was designed by the architect Sir William Bruce and built in 1687 for Sir James Dick, the Roman Catholic Provost of Edinburgh. Its predecessor, Priestfield House, had been burnt down in an anti-Catholic student protest in the 1670s, so Sir James considered it wise to alter the original name, which derived from the land having been donated to the Cistercian monastery of Holm Cultram, now within modern Cumbria, by King David I around 1153.

Sir Alexander Dick (born Alexander Cunyngham), grandson of Sir

Carolina, Lady Nairne (1766-1845). From Francis Watt's Book of Edinburgh Anecdote *(T N Foulis, 1912).*

James Dick and President of the Royal College of Physicians of Edinburgh from 1756-1763, lived at Prestonfield. He was visited there by Dr Johnson and James Boswell on their visit to Scotland in 1773. In the following year, Sir Alexander was awarded a gold medal by the Society of Arts for his successful introduction of rhubarb to Scotland. Among Sir Alexander's other illustrious visitors were Benjamin Franklin, one of the Founding Fathers of the United States, David Hume, the historian and philosopher, and Allan Ramsay, the painter.

The Dick-Cunyngham family, as they later styled themselves, continued to live in Prestonfield House until the house became a five-star hotel in the 1960s.

The coastal part of Duddingston parish later developed into the town of Portobello, which takes its name from a single house built in the eighteenth century. According to the *New Statistical Account*, this small cottage was constructed by a retired sailor, who had served with Vice-

Admiral Edward Vernon in Panama, and he apparently named it Porto Bello in commemoration of the British capture of that town in 1739.

In the late eighteenth century, clay was discovered beside the Figgate Burn, which flows into the Firth of Forth at Portobello. A brick and tile works was established, followed by an earthenware pottery factory, leading to a rise in the local population. In 1833, Portobello and the neighbouring district of Joppa, became a burgh, with glass, lead, paper, soap and mustard being manufactured there. In 1896, the burgh of Portobello was absorbed into Edinburgh.

The beach at Portobello was used for drill practice by the Edinburgh Light Horse in the early nineteenth century, and King George IV reviewed cavalrymen and Highlanders on Portobello sands during his 1822 visit to Scotland. This was the first visit to Scotland by a reigning British monarch since 1650.

From the early 1800s, Portobello enjoyed a reputation as a bathing place, and it had become a crowded seaside resort by the mid-twentieth century, with a promenade (from 1876), pier (from 1871-1917), heated outdoor swimming pool and multi-level diving boards (from 1936-1984), permanent funfair (until 2007), two amusement arcades, and ice-cream parlours.

Tanya Arcari, whose family ran an ice-cream shop at 99 Portobello High Street for more than eighty years, claims her grandfather, Stephen, invented the popular '99' in the 1920s by putting a chocolate flake into an ice-cream cone.

'Portie' was popular not only among Edinburgh people, but also with those from Scotland's west coast, who came during the Glasgow Fair fortnight in July. Portobello's success declined in the late twentieth century, as continental holidays became cheaper, but the area is now in the process of restoring its former fortunes as a holiday resort.

6.8 The parishes of Ratho, Currie, Kirkliston and Dalmeny (including Queensferry)

In 1975, fifty-five years after the previous major boundary change, the City of Edinburgh's boundary moved significantly to the west. This change brought into the city not only the parishes of Ratho and Currie in Midlothian, but also Dalmeny (including the burgh of Queensferry) in West Lothian. Kirkliston, which had been mainly in West Lothian and partly in Midlothian, was also incorporated into Edinburgh.

Ratho

The parish of Ratho was surrounded by Kirkliston and Corstorphine parishes on the north side, by Currie on the east, and by Kirknewton on the west. The name may be of British origin, referring to 'forts', a 'monastic enclosure' or a 26-acre holding. Villages in the parish were Ratho itself and Bonnington.

Large houses in the parish of Ratho included Haltoun or Hatton House, which dates back at least as far as the late fourteenth century. The house was sold in 1377 to the Lauder family, in whose possession it remained until it passed by marriage to the Maitland family (Earls of Lauderdale) in 1652. The original tower house was altered over the years into a grand country house, which was owned by the Maitlands until 1792. Subsequently, Haltoun House had a number of proprietors until it was unfortunately destroyed by fire in February 1952.

Dalmahoy House was designed by William Adam and built in 1725 for George Dalrymple, a younger son of the Earl of Stair. Prior to that, the estate belonged to the Dalmahoy family. In 1750, the house was sold to James Douglas, 14th Earl of Morton. Alterations and extensions were made to the house in the eighteenth, nineteenth and twentieth centuries. Since 1927, Dalmahoy House has been a hotel, with golf courses in its grounds.

Currie

The parish of Currie was surrounded by the parishes of Corstorphine in the north-east, Colinton in the east, Penicuik in the south-east, (West) Linton in Peeblesshire in the south, Ratho in the north-west, Kirknewton in the west, and Mid Calder in the south-west. The parish name probably derives from the British (Old Welsh) 'curi', meaning 'a hollow'.

By the nineteenth century, there were only two villages in the parish: Currie itself and Balerno (from the Gaelic 'bail(e) àirneach', meaning 'farm with the sloe bushes'). According to the Reverend Robert Jamieson, writing around 1845 in the *New Statistical Account*, Currie's population had been much larger previously, and several 'populous villages' had entirely disappeared, with the upper parts of the parish then much more thinly populated than in the past.

Regarding longevity among the local people, the Reverend Jamieson notes that:

'The inhabitants of Currie are rather famed for being long-lived. William Ritchie died at the age of 108. His son, Adam Ritchie, exceeded the age of 100.

'About fifty years ago William Napier, Balerno, died at the age of 112. William was an excellent pedestrian, and was frequently victor at the Lammas races, formerly a favourite pastime in rural districts, where the peasantry met and entered the lists to contest for small prizes. This man, on one occasion, when running the "bruze" at a wedding [an informal race at country weddings], not only distanced his competitors, but outstripped a person mounted on a hunting horse, who rode as arbiter of the race. He was through life noted for his prodigious muscular power; and it is mentioned in evidence of his athletic frame, that he was in the habit of providing grass for his cow daily, by cutting it with the scythe, when he was upwards of 100.

'John Dawson died at Nether Currie in 1821 at the advanced age of 100. Mr Thomas Craig of Riccarton died at the age of 86, having been eighty-four years proprietor. A few years ago, six members of the Malleny family survived, whose united ages averaged 81 years.'

Large houses in the parish of Currie included:

• **Riccarton House** was a tower house built in 1508 by the Wardlaw family, then sold in 1610 to the Craigs, who extended it in 1621. The house was remodelled in the Scottish baronial style from 1823-1827 for Sir James Gibson-Craig. Riccarton House was used as an army base during the Second World War, then as a resettlement camp for ex-prisoners of war, and finally as the headquarters of the Royal Artillery 3rd Anti-Aircraft Group. The house was demolished in 1956 as it was judged structurally unsafe. In 1969, the grounds were bought by the Heriot-Watt University (see Chapter 16.2) as the site of its new suburban campus.
• **Curriehill Castle** was bought by Sir John Skene in 1594, who was created Lord Curriehill. In 1656, Skene's son sold the castle to Samuel Johnstone, but by the eighteenth century it was in ruins. John Marshall, an Edinburgh lawyer, bought the estate in the nineteenth century and had Curriehill House built in 1856. Both the

house and remains of the castle were replaced by a housing estate in the 1970s.

- **Ravelrig House** in Balerno was built in the late sixteenth century and considerably extended in the seventeenth. The building was redeveloped in the late eighteenth and late nineteenth centuries and doubled in size during the 1920s. In 1948, Ravelrig House was bought by the charity Barnardo's, initially as a home for babies and toddlers, and then became a mixed home from September 1971 to February 1975. The building was reopened in November 1977 as a home for children with physical and learning disabilities, but Barnardo's no longer runs children's homes. More recently, Ravelrig House was damaged by fire and, together with its stables and cottages, it has since been converted to eleven luxury dwellings (six within the main house).
- **Baberton House** (formerly called Kilbaberton) was built at least as early as 1622 for Sir James Murray (Master of Works to James VI) and is now used as offices for Cruden Homes in the East of Scotland. Part of the Baberton estate has been converted into Baberton Golf Club, which claims to be the birthplace of the steel-shafted golf club.

The Reverend Jamieson also mentions in the *New Statistical Account* (without supplying names) that:

'some families of inferior rank have been long resident in the parish, as for instance, the present tenant on the farm of East Mill, with his father and grandfather, have been farmers on the estate of Malleny for upwards of 120 years. The present tenants on the farms of Harelaw, Kenleith, and Balleny, with their progenitors, have held land on the same estate upwards of 100 years, and their ancestors, as well as those of the Cuninghams of Balerno, have resided within the parish for three or four centuries.'

Kirkliston

Most of the parish of Kirkliston (the western part) was located in the county of West Lothian, while a smaller eastern area lay in Midlothian. The parish was surrounded by Abercorn and Dalmeny to the north, a detached part of Dalmeny (the eastern part of which was incorporated in Kirkliston in 1891), Ecclesmachan and Uphall to the west,

Kirknewton and Ratho to the south, and Cramond and Corstorphine to the east.

Stuart Harris, in *The Place Names of Edinburgh*, derives the name of the parish from the 'kirk' (or 'church') of 'liss' (British for an ancient ruin) 'ton' ('farm'). The main villages in the parish are Kirkliston itself and Winchburgh. The Reverend Adam Duncan Tait, writes in the *New Statistical Account* that:

> 'The great increase of population [of 534 people] since 1811 is supposed to have been owing to the extraordinary number of labourers, chiefly Irishmen, who were employed in the parish in the years 1818-1821, in the construction of the Union Canal, many of whom became, from that time, settled inhabitants.
>
> 'The number of farms in the parish is 30; the number of farm servants, statedly employed in the management of these, is about 140. There are 11 wrights; 9 smiths; 5 tailors; 8 shoemakers; 5 grocers; 2 candle-makers; 4 bakers. There is one medical gentleman in the parish.'

Large estates and houses in the parish of Kirkliston included:

- The **Clifton Hall** estate dates back to the early thirteenth century, when Sir Henry Graham gave a charter of the lands to his cousin, David Graham. In the sixteenth century, the owner was Thomas Macalzean, who was elected Provost of Edinburgh in 1561. His daughter, Euphame Macalzean, was executed for witchcraft on Castle Hill in Edinburgh in June 1591. A century later, Archibald Douglas became the owner. Douglas had fought against the Covenanters under Sir Tam Dalyell of the Binns, who was appointed commander-in-chief in Scotland by King Charles II in 1666. In 1703, the Clifton Hall estate was bought by Lieutenant-Colonel George Wishart, who was created a baronet in 1706 by Queen Anne. The estate was sold in 1761 to Thomas Gibson of Pentland, and passed by the marriage of his granddaughter to Sir Alexander Charles Maitland, who fought in the American Revolutionary War (or War of Independence). In the early twentieth century, the estate was bought by St Cuthbert's Co-operative Society of Edinburgh, which kept the estate farms until 1957, but sold Clifton Hall house (built in 1857) and its grounds to

Argyll Lindsay, a Leith grain merchant. He, in turn, sold them to Richard Killick, who founded Clifton Hall School in 1930.

- In the fifteenth century, Duncan Dundas, Lord Lyon King of Arms, bought **Newliston House**, which passed by marriage in the seventeenth century to John Dalrymple, 1st Earl of Stair. After the death of the Second Earl, Newliston was sold in 1747 to a London merchant named Roger Hog. Around forty years later, the present house was designed by William Adam for Hog's son, whose descendants still live there today.

- The present **Ingliston House** was built in 1846 for William Mitchell-Innes of Parson's Green and Bangour, in the Scottish baronial style. The Ingliston estate had been granted to the Knights Templar in 1134 by King David I, and passed to the Knights of St John in 1312. Later owners included: James Inglis in 1631; George Smollet in 1710; the Second Earl of Hopetoun in 1744; James Gibson (later known as Sir James Gibson-Craig) in 1801; Robert Stewart in 1862; Duncan Macpherson of Glen Doll in 1887; William C P Brown, chairman of Heart of Midlothian FC (see Chapter 4.7) in 1934; and the Royal Highland and Agricultural Society of Scotland in 1958. Since then, the estate has been the site of the Royal Highland Showground.

Dalmeny (including Queensferry)

The coastal parish of Dalmeny was bounded on the east by Cramond, on the south by Kirkliston and on the west by the parish of Abercorn. The western part of a detached area of the parish of Dalmeny was transferred in 1891 to Ecclesmachan parish, and the eastern part to the parish of Kirkliston.

According to W J Watson's *The Celtic Place-Names of Scotland*, the name of Dalmeny (earlier Dummany) is probably derived from 'din meyni' in the British language, meaning a 'stone fort'. The present Dalmeny parish church building dates from the twelfth century, and may be built on a pre-Christian burial mound. A seventh-century coffin stone was found near the church door.

Barnbougle Castle, originally a thirteenth-century tower house and the seat of the Mowbray family, was sold in 1662 to the Primrose family (who became Earls of Rosebery in 1703). Watson suggests the name may derive from the British 'pren bugail', meaning 'herdsman's tree'. The castle was reconstructed in 1881 to house the library of

Archibald Primrose, 5th Earl of Rosebery, who was Prime Minister of the United Kingdom from 1894-1895. Dalmeny House was built for the Earls of Rosebery in 1817, in Tudor Gothic style, to replace Barnbougle Castle.

The original Dundas Castle was built by James Dundas about 1416 as a defensive residence. The modern castle dates from 1818, and was designed by the architect William Burn. The castle had belonged to the Dundas family for more than 450 years when it was sold to Stewart Clark, the owner of a textile company, in whose family's possession the castle remains.

The largest settlement in Dalmeny parish was Queensferry, which takes its name from Queen Margaret (wife of Malcolm III), who improved the existing ferry by endowing it with boats, hostels and free passage for the poor and pilgrims. Queensferry became a burgh before 1300 and a royal burgh in 1636. (See Appendix A4.6.) The only other village within the parish is Dalmeny itself.

PART TWO – EDINBURGH'S RECORDS

Chapter 7

BIRTHS, MARRIAGES AND DEATHS IN EDINBURGH

7.1 Statutory registers of births, marriages and deaths (civil registration)

The first records you should consult to trace your Edinburgh ancestors are those of births, marriages and deaths, working back to create your family tree. From 1 January 1855, these events were recorded by the General Register Office for Scotland (GROS) in the statutory registers of births, marriages and deaths. This civil registration took the place of the baptism, marriage and burial records entered in the Church of Scotland parish registers, although these events have also continued to be recorded in the registers.

The birth, marriage and death records of Scotland may begin seventeen years later than those for England and Wales, but the Scottish records contain more information. Because of this factor, and their availability online, you can expect to trace your Edinburgh ancestors back to 1855 quickly and without much difficulty.

In the first year (1855), Scottish civil registration records contained even more information. Both the registrars and the public, however, found that it was too much of an effort to provide all of the information initially collected, so less detail was asked for in 1856, although some categories were restored in 1861.

7.2 Birth records

The Scottish statutory register of births records:

- When and where the child was born;
- The hour of its birth;
- The child's name;
- Its sex;
- The forename, surname and occupation of the father;
- The forename, surname and maiden surname of the mother;
- The date and place of the parents' marriage (1855 and 1861 onwards);
- The signature, description and residence of the person who provided the birth information;
- The date and place of registration, plus the registrar's signature.

In 1855, the following additional information was collected:

- The baptismal name (if this was different to the official name);
- The father's age;
- The father's birthplace;

Statutory birth record, 1861. (Reproduced with the kind permission of the Registrar General for Scotland.)

861 DONALDSON, DAVID SINCLAIR (Statutory Births 684/01 0015)

rown Copyright. Image was generated at 15 December 2010 12:14

- The numbers of girls and boys in the family still living, and the numbers of each who were deceased;
- The mother's age;
- The mother's birthplace;
- The position of the newborn child in the family, such as 'her 3rd child' (although this was not officially required).

It's very useful to find the date and place of the parents' marriage, as this can make it easier to go back a generation. Beware of treating this information as gospel, however. My own great-grandparents William Brockman Stewart and Agnes Craig married on 16 June 1884, but their first child Mary Alicia had been born on 16 May of that year. On the birth certificates of William and Agnes's next five children born within the marriage, they gave the date of their marriage as 16 May, Mary Alicia's birth date – but for some reason left the year as 1884.

The extra 1855 information can be very helpful, so it's worth looking for someone in the family who may have been born in that year, even if he or she isn't a direct ancestor.

7.3 Marriage records
The Scottish statutory marriage registers record:

- The date and place of the marriage;
- According to which type of ceremony they married;
- The names and signatures of the bride and groom;
- Their ages;
- Where they lived at the time of their marriage;
- Their occupations;
- Their prior marital status;
- Their prior relationship (if any);
- The forenames, surnames and occupations of the couple's fathers;
- The forenames, surnames and maiden surnames of the couple's mothers;
- The signature of the officiating minister;
- The signatures of the witnesses.

The additional 1855 information includes:

Statutory marriage record, 1906. (Reproduced with the kind permission of the Registrar General for Scotland.)

- The usual addresses of the bride and groom, as well as their present addresses;
- If the groom is a widower or the bride a widow, whether this is his or her second or third marriage;
- The number of children born during any previous marriages, both living and dead;
- The dates and places of birth of the bride and groom.

Unlike the Scottish birth and death records, which contain the signatures of the informants, the Scottish marriage records simply have '(Signed)' and the names written out by the registrar. Also in contrast to English marriage records, those for Scotland give not only the names of the fathers of the bride and groom, but also the forenames and maiden surnames of their mothers, which is very helpful.

Scotland had no civil marriage ceremonies before 1 July 1940. Until then, couples had either a regular marriage performed in a church by a minister or an irregular marriage by declaration before witnesses, such as those carried out over the anvil at Gretna Green and Lamberton Toll.

It's worth searching the records to see whether any of your ancestors were married in Edinburgh, even if they didn't live there. I have found four such marriages in my own ancestry: one recorded in the statutory register in 1870, and three in the parish registers in 1806, 1811 and 1813 (the marriages of three sets of great-great-great-grandparents).

The marriage of Alexander Gow and Helen Gow in Edinburgh in 1806 may have been frowned on in their home parish of Blair Atholl, as they were probably cousins; and my great-grandparents Joseph Tait and Jemima Munro may have married quietly in Leith in 1870, as Jemima was pregnant at the time. Alexander Stewart from Skye and Ann Allan from Caithness married in Edinburgh in 1813, as Alexander was stationed in Edinburgh Castle with his regiment. I have no idea why George Walker and Joan Brodie married in the capital in April 1811, however. It may have had something to do with the fact that Joan's widowed father, James Brodie, was set to marry an Agnes Walker in August 1811.

7.4 Death records
The Scottish statutory death registers record:

- The forename and surname of the deceased;
- His or her occupation and marital status;
- When and where the death took place;
- His or her sex and age;
- The forename, surname and occupation of the deceased's father;
- The forename, surname and maiden surname of the deceased's mother;
- The cause of death, duration of the illness and the name of the doctor attending (if any);
- The signature, relationship and address of the informant (if not living in the house in which the death took place);
- When and where the death was registered and the registrar's signature.

Page 439

1936. DEATHS in the DISTRICT of LEITH in the CITY of EDINBURGH

No.	Name and Surname. Rank or Profession, and whether Single, Married, or Widowed.	When and Where Died.	Sex.	Age.	Name, Surname, and Rank or Profession of Father. Name, and Maiden Surname of Mother.	Cause of Death, Duration of Disease, and Medical Attendant by whom certified.	Signature and Qualification of Informant, and Residence, if out of the House in which the Death occurred.	When and Where Registered, and Signature of Registrar.
1315	Catherine Smith Married to Andrew Smith House Painter (Retired)	1936. November Twentyninth 4h. 5m. am. Caroline Park Granton Edinburgh.	F	75 years	William McDonald Butler (deceased) Helen McDonald M.S. Anderson (deceased)	Broncho Pneumonia 6 days. As cert. by J. Colin Baird M.B.	Andrew Smith Son. 16 Darnell Road Leith	1936. November 30th At Leith Thos M Belfer Registrar.
1316	Agnes May Maulay Married to Edward Francis Maulay Gas Works Labourer	1936. November Twentyeighth 6h am. Eastern General Hospital Leith (usual residence: 41 Blackfriars Street, Edinburgh)	F	43 years	Thomas Crilley General Labourer (deceased) Catherine Crilley M.S. Bagan (deceased)	Lobar Pneumonia Coronary Thrombosis Chronic Myocarditis Adenoma of Abdominal Aorta As cert. by Alex Jungfaldt L.R.C.P.S.	Edward F. F. Maulay Widower 41 Blackfriars Street Edinburgh	1936. November 30th At Leith Geo D M Bulloch Asmr. Registrar. J M2
1317	George Robert Tait Manufacturing Furrier Married to Elizabeth Watt	1936. November Twentyeighth 11h. 40m. PM. Eastern General Hospital Leith (usual residence: 35 St Patrick Square Edinburgh)	M	62 years	Joseph Tait Joiner (deceased) Jemima Tait M.S. Munro (deceased)	Chronic Myocarditis Hemiplegia Hypespinea Chronic Gastritis As cert. by L.R.C.P.S.	John Tait Son. 17 Union Place Edinburgh	1936. November 30th At Leith Thos M Belfer Registrar.

D

Thos M Belfer Registrar.

Statutory death record, 1936. (Reproduced with the kind permission of the Registrar General for Scotland.)

In 1855, the following information was also required:

- Where the deceased was born, and how long he or she had been living in the current district;
- The name of the deceased's spouse (although this information was not specifically asked for after 1855, it was normally given from 1861 onwards);
- The names of the deceased's children in order of birth, together with their ages. For children who had died, their year of death and age at death were given;
- When the attending doctor last saw the deceased;
- Where the deceased was buried, and the undertaker's signature. (This information was given from 1855-1860.)

Although it can be very helpful to find the names of the deceased person's parents on the death record, you shouldn't put too much faith in those names being 100 per cent correct. Sometimes only one name is given, or none at all.

The death year supplied for a child of the deceased may also be incorrect. On my great-great-great-grandmother Helen Gow's 1855 death record, her daughter Christian (my great-great-grandmother) is shown as 'Dec. at 40 in 1852'. However, Christian's husband John MacKenzie is already shown as a widower in the 1851 census.

7.5 Register of Corrected Entries
Any amendments, additions or corrections to birth, marriage or death records were entered in the Register of Corrected Entries (RCE). 'RCE' or 'Reg. Cor. Ent.' would be written in the left-hand margin of the original record, plus the volume number, page number and date.

7.6 Minor Records
The so-called 'Minor Records' are the records of births, marriages and deaths that took place outside Scotland, in cases where (as the National Records of Scotland puts it) 'it appears that one of the child's parents, or the deceased person, was usually resident in Scotland.'

The Minor Records are:

- The Air Register (of births and deaths) from 1948;
- Consular Returns (of births and deaths) from 1914;
- Foreign Returns (of births, marriages and deaths) from 1860-1965;
- High Commission Returns (of births and deaths) from 1964;
- Foreign marriages without the presence of a British Consular Officer from 1947;
- The Marine Register (of births and deaths) from 1855;
- Service Returns (of births, marriages and deaths) from 1881-1959;
- War Returns (of deaths) for the South African (Boer) War;
- War Returns (of deaths) for the First World War;
- War Returns (of deaths) for the Second World War;
- Marriages solemnised by army chaplains.

7.7 Divorce records
While Scotland was still a Roman Catholic country, divorce was practically unknown, and it was only after the state religion changed to Protestantism in 1560 that divorce became possible on the grounds of adultery and, thirteen years later, of desertion. From 1560, divorce was dealt with by the Court of Session, and from 1563, by the Commissary

Court of Edinburgh. In 1830, in theory, and from 1835 in practice, responsibility for divorce returned to the Court of Session.

During the twentieth century, anti-social behaviour, cruelty and non-cohabitation were added to adultery and desertion as grounds for divorce, and from 1976, divorce by mutual consent became possible for the first time. From 1984, local sheriff courts could hear divorce cases, and nearly all of Scotland's divorce cases (around 12,000 a year) are now heard locally.

7.8 Where are these records located?

You can view the statutory birth, marriage and death records at the ScotlandsPeople Centre in Edinburgh (see Appendix 2). If you live in or near the capital, or if you happen to be visiting, then this is the cheapest way to look at the records. For most people, however, the only realistic option is online access to the records, via the official ScotlandsPeople pay-per-view website, www.scotlandspeople.gov.uk (see Appendix 1).

ScotlandsPeople lets you view and download images of many different Scottish records. For civil registration births, marriages and deaths, there are cut-off points of 100, 75 and 50 years respectively, and these move forward a year each January. At the time of writing (the spring of 2015), you can therefore view and download birth records up to the end of 1914, marriage records to the end of 1939 and death records to the end of 1964.

To view a more recent record (including any of the minor records), you'll need to order a certificate through ScotlandsPeople, where online indexes currently extend right up to the end of 2013.

The National Records of Scotland holds all but the most recent Scottish divorce records, which are mostly listed or indexed and relatively accessible. The NRS points out that traditionally a married woman retained her maiden name in Scotland, and that you should bear this in mind when searching for records.

You can search for records of Scottish divorces using the NRS online catalogue, at http://tinyurl.com/NRSonlinecat, specifying 'divorce' and the surname of either of the parties. This will give you the document reference number, which you can then quote to the NRS (see Appendix 2), where staff will give you the estimated cost of copying and sending you the divorce papers.

Chapter 8

LISTS OF EDINBURGH'S PEOPLE

8.1 The 1755 Webster Census

An unofficial census of Scotland was carried out in 1755 by the ministers of all the parishes in Scotland, on the instructions of Dr Alexander Webster, Moderator of the General Assembly of the Church of Scotland. You can read and download the results of this census (which does not supply names) at the National Records of Scotland website: www.nrscotland.gov.uk/research/guides/census-records/webster's-census-of-1755.

Webster's figures for the parishes within the present-day City of Edinburgh area are:

Canongate	4,500
Colinton	792
Corstorphine	995
Cramond	1,455
Currie	1,227
Dalmeny	1,103
Duddingston	989
Edinburgh	31,122
Kirkliston	1,461
Liberton	2,793
Leith, North	2,205
Leith, South	7,200
Queensferry	451
Ratho	930
St Cuthbert's	12,193
TOTAL	69,416

8.2 Official censuses 1801-2011

An official census was first taken in Scotland in 1801 and every ten years thereafter (apart from in 1941, because of the Second World War). The 1931 census of Scotland is still in existence, unlike that for England and Wales which was destroyed in 1942 during a fire (unrelated to enemy bombing).

As in the English and Welsh censuses, enumerators were not required to record individual names until 1841. Although some of the enumerators did list names in the 1801-1831 censuses, there are no such records surviving for the present-day City of Edinburgh area. The detailed records of the censuses up to and including 1911 are already open to the public, with the 1921 census due to be released in 2022.

The various censuses took place on the dates below, when the population figures for the Edinburgh area were:

1801	10 March	82,560 (including Leith)
1811	27 May	102,987 (including Leith)
1821	28 May	138,235 (including Leith)
1831	29 May	161,909 (including Leith)
1841	6 June	138,182 (Leith 28,159; Portobello 3,588; Queensferry 721)
1851	30 March	160,302 (Leith 30,919; Portobello 3,497; Queensferry 1,195)
1861	7 April	168,098 (Leith 33,530; Portobello 4,366; Queensferry 1,230)
1871	2 April	196,500 (Leith 44,277; Portobello 5,481; Queensferry 1,521)
1881	3 April	228,190 (Leith 58,193; Portobello 6,793; Queensferry 1,676)
1891	5 April	261,261 (Leith 67,660; Portobello 8,181; Queensferry 1,531)
1901	31 March	298,069 (Leith 76,667; Portobello 9,180; Queensferry 1,845)
1911	2 April	320,315 (Leith 80,489; Queensferry 2,812)
1921	19 June	420,281 (Queensferry 2,193)
1931	26 April	438,998 (Queensferry 1,798)
1941	————	(no census taken)
1951	8 April	466,761

1961	23 April	468,361
1971	25 April	453,585
1981	5 April	425,256
1991	21 April	418,914
2001	29 April	448,624
2011	27 March	476,626

Although Portobello was incorporated into Edinburgh in 1896, its population was still shown separately in 1901.

In 1911, Leith was the seventh most populous burgh in Scotland, following Glasgow, Edinburgh, Dundee, Aberdeen, Govan (part of Glasgow from 1912) and Paisley. Leith was incorporated into Edinburgh in 1920.

8.3 The 1841 census

Unlike later censuses, the 1841 census of Scotland doesn't list exact places of birth, as is also the case with the censuses taken in England and Wales during that year. The question asked in the Scottish census was 'if born in Scotland, state whether in county or otherwise' or 'whether foreigner, or whether born in England or Ireland'.

There was no question about relationships between members of a household in the 1841 census, so beware of assuming that a man and a woman who are around the same age and share the same surname are necessarily husband and wife – they might be brother and sister, or cousins. You may be lucky, however, as I was when looking for my three times great-grandparents James and Catherine Ross (nee Miller) in the 1841 census. The enumerator had listed them (in the parish of Banchory Ternan in Kincardineshire) as 'James Ross' and 'Catherine Miller (wife)'. There are six women listed as 'wife' on the two pages shown on that particular census image, three of whom are recorded under their maiden surnames.

Also, unlike later censuses, ages of anyone over fifteen were supposed to be rounded down to the nearest five years, so an age of 'twenty' in an 1841 census return may indicate a person aged from twenty to twenty-four. The enumerators didn't always follow their instructions, however, so the ages of James and Catherine Ross in the above example are shown as 'forty-seven' and 'forty-nine' respectively.

The information recorded in the 1841 census includes:

- Place (village, street, etc);
- Houses – uninhabited or building;
- Houses – inhabited;
- Names of each person who abode there in the preceding night;
- Age;
- Sex;
- Profession, trade, employment or of independent means;
- Whether born in the same county;
- Whether a foreigner or born in England or Ireland.

8.4 The 1851-1911 censuses

From 1851 onwards, the census enumerators were required to find out each occupant's exact age and his or her relationship to the head of the household. In addition, a person's parish and county of birth were asked for, if he or she had been born in Scotland. If not, then only 'England' (which included Wales), 'Ireland' or the name of their country of origin were required. In many cases, however, more detailed information was given.

More information was asked for over the years, with some questions being particular to Scotland. In 1861 and 1871, for instance, people were asked how many children aged between five and fifteen years old were attending school, and in 1871, how many children were being educated at home. The number of rooms with windows in the house was required information from 1861 onwards, and there was also a question on whether individuals could speak Gaelic or Gaelic and English from 1891.

Although the 1881 census had no official question on Gaelic, the enumerators were asked to carry out a trial run to find the number of Gaelic speakers. In 1881, my great-great-grandparents Robert and Margery Munro were living in the township of Borgue in the parish of Latheron in Caithness. A 'G' in brackets, meaning Gaelic, has been put after the family's birthplaces, and this ties in with 'G&E', Gaelic and English, as the family members' answer to the Gaelic question in 1891.

Census return, 1911. (Reproduced with the kind permission of the Registrar General for Scotland)

The information given in the censuses from 1851 (or later) includes:

- Name of street, place or road, and name or number of house;
- Name and surname of each person who lived in the house;
- Relationship to head of family;
- Marital status;
- Age;
- Sex;
- Rank, profession or occupation;
- Where born;
- Whether blind, or deaf and dumb;
- Houses – uninhabited or building (from 1861);
- Houses – inhabited (from 1861);
- Number of rooms with one or more windows (from 1861);
- Number of children from five to fifteen attending school (1861 and 1871 only);
- Number of children from five to fifteen being educated at home (1871 only);

- Whether imbecile or idiot (from 1871);
- Whether lunatic (from 1871);
- Gaelic or English (from 1891, with trial in 1881);
- Employer (from 1891);
- Employed (from 1891);
- Working on own account, i.e. self-employed (from 1891);
- Working at home (from 1901);
- Number of persons in house (from 1911);
- Duration of marriage (from 1911);
- Children born alive (from 1911);
- Children still living (from 1911);
- Industry or service (from 1911);
- Nationality if born in a foreign country (from 1911).

8.5 Where are the census records located?

As with the birth, marriage and death records, you can view the census returns in person at the ScotlandsPeople Centre in Edinburgh (see Appendix 2), or online at several websites.

Images of the returns from the 1841-1911 censuses of Scotland are online only at ScotlandsPeople, www.scotlandspeople.gov.uk (see Appendix 1). You can, however, view transcriptions of the 1841-1901 censuses at the subscription sites Ancestry.co.uk, www.ancestry.co.uk, and Findmypast.co.uk, www.findmypast.co.uk. The 1911 census of Scotland, however, is available online only at ScotlandsPeople.

In addition, transcriptions of the 1841 and 1851 censuses for all of the Midlothian parishes are online at the FreeCEN volunteer project website, www.freecen.org.uk, as are those for West Lothian for the 1841 census.

8.6 Directories

The earliest Edinburgh directories were compiled and issued in the late eighteenth century by private publishers, who often gathered information in the course of their work with registry offices, housing agencies, printers or the police. In 1805, the Post Office began to publish directories for Edinburgh, collecting the information via its letter carriers, and by the late nineteenth century, it had become the major publisher of Scottish directories.

Up to around 1850, most directories contained the names and

addresses of only the 'principal inhabitants' of an area (i.e. those who could afford to pay the fee for an entry), as well as tradesmen, shopkeepers and farmers. The National Library of Scotland (NLS), which holds many directories in its collections, points out that employees, small traders, craftsmen, labourers and servants are rarely found in the lists. Nor are women, because only the head of a household would normally be recorded.

More than 700 Scottish Directories (mostly published by the Post Office) may be viewed free of charge at the NLS website http://digital.nls.uk/directories. For Edinburgh, the site holds 127 directories.

Early Directories
The following directories, now available online, were originally published by private publishers:

- *Williamson's Directory for the City of Edinburgh, Canongate, Leith and Suburbs from 25 May 1773 to 25 May 1774* (in a facsimile reprint published in 1889);
- *Williamson's Directory for the City of Edinburgh, Canongate, Leith and Suburbs from 25 May 1774 to 25 May 1775;*
- *Williamson's Directory for the City of Edinburgh, Canongate, Leith and Suburbs from 25 May 1775 to 25 May 1776;*
- *Williamson's Directory for the City of Edinburgh, Canongate, Leith and Suburbs from June 1784 to June 1785;*
- *Williamson's Edinburgh Directory from June 1790 to June 1792;*
- *Aitchison's Edinburgh Directory from July 1797 to July 1798;*
- *Aitchison's Edinburgh and Leith Directory to July 1800;*
- *Aitchison's Edinburgh and Leith Directory to July 1801;*
- *Denovan & Co.'s Edinburgh and Leith Directory from July 1804 to July 1805.*

Post Office Directories
The NLS has also made available online over 100 Post Office Directories, from the *Post Office Annual Directory of Edinburgh and Leith from Whitsunday 1805 to Whitsunday 1806* to the *Post Office Edinburgh and Leith Directory 1911-1912.*

Commercial directories

In addition to the Post Office Directories, the NLS has put some other nineteenth century directories online:

- *Gray's Annual Directory ... of Edinburgh, Leith and Suburbs 1832-33;*
- *Gray's Annual Directory 1833-34 ... of Edinburgh and its Vicinity;*
- *Gray's Annual Directory 1834-35 ... of Edinburgh and its Vicinity;*
- *Gray's Annual Directory and Edinburgh Almanac 1836-37;*
- *Gray's Annual Directory and Edinburgh Almanac 1837-38;*

- *New Edinburgh, Leith and County Directory 1867-68;*
- *New Edinburgh, Leith and County Business Directory 1868-69;*
- *New Edinburgh, Leith and County Directory 1869-70;*
- *New Edinburgh, Leith and County Household Directory 1868-69.*

8.7 Telephone directories

You'll find a collection of digitised UK telephone directories from 1880-1984 online at the subscription website Ancestry.co.uk, www.ancestry.co.uk. If you can't find a person through the online search, try browsing a directory to locate their entry, as you would in a printed copy.

8.8 Valuation rolls from 1855 onwards

There are earlier land valuation rolls (see Land Tax in Chapter 14), but a uniform valuation of landed property in Scotland didn't take place until the Land Valuation (Scotland) Act of 1854. Valuation rolls (except for businesses) were replaced in 1989 with the introduction of Community Charge (the 'Poll Tax'), where the tax was on individuals instead of properties. This was carried out a year earlier than in England and Wales. Community Charge was, in turn, replaced by Council Tax in 1993.

A valuation roll is not as helpful to the family historian as a census return (as the valuation roll provides only a heads-of-household listing), but it will enable you to discover the year in which your ancestor moved from one address to another. (For annual rents below £4, tenants were usually grouped together as 'small tenants' or 'sundry tenants'.) You may also discover that some of your ancestors once owned land or houses that you had been unaware of.

A typical valuation roll includes:

- Description (e.g. 'house and land');
- Situation (e.g. street name and number);
- Proprietor;
- Tenant;
- Occupier (this is usually the tenant, but may be the proprietor);
- Yearly Rent or Value.

Valuation record, 1920. (Crown Copyright, National Records of Scotland, VR100/378, page 282.)

The valuation records from 1855-1989 are held by the National Records of Scotland, and those up to 1957/58 have been digitised and made available in the NRS search rooms as 'virtual volumes'.

The NRS has compiled an index of the valuation rolls for the years 1855/56, 1865/66, 1875/76, 1885/86, 1895/96, 1905/06, 1915/1916,

1920/21, 1925/26, 1930/31, 1935/36, 1940/41, 1945/46, 1950/51 and 1955/56. The rolls for those years are being added to the pay-per-view ScotlandsPeople website, www.scotlandspeople.gov.uk.

The rolls from 1957/58 onwards, the Community Charge registers and Council Tax valuation lists are also held by the NRS.

8.9 Online catalogues

You can try searching the National Records of Scotland online catalogue, at http://tinyurl.com/NRSonlinecat, for the many records held by the NRS. In addition, the Scottish Archive Network online catalogue, at www.scan.org.uk/catalogue, lets you search for records held by various other archives in Scotland.

By entering a particular archive code in the appropriate search field, you can narrow your search to a specific archive, such as the Edinburgh-based archives listed below:

Archive	Code
Edinburgh City Archives	GB236
Edinburgh College of Art	GB2028
Edinburgh University Library, Special Collections	GB237
Heriot-Watt University Archive	GB582
Lothian Health Services Archive	GB239
Midlothian Council Archives	GB584
National Library of Scotland	GB233
National Records of Scotland	GB234
National Trust for Scotland, Edinburgh	GB1873
Royal Bank of Scotland Archives	GB1502
Royal College of Surgeons of Edinburgh	GB779
Scottish Catholic Archives	GB240
Scottish National Gallery of Modern Art	GB2610

The National Register of Archives for Scotland contains more than 4,200 surveys of private papers, including the records of landed estates, businesses, law firms, societies and private individuals. You can search the register at http://tinyurl.com/NRAScotland.

Chapter 9

THE CHURCH IN EDINBURGH

The Church of Scotland (informally known as the 'Kirk') was part of the Roman Catholic Church until 1560, formally adopting a Presbyterian structure in 1592, which consisted of a number of courts. Bishops and archbishops were abolished, but re-introduced in the early seventeenth century by King James VI, by then also King James I of England.

Many people in Scotland were unhappy when James's son, King Charles I, ordered the use of an Anglican-style prayer book in the Scottish Church, and in 1638, a 'National Covenant' was signed at Greyfriars Church in Edinburgh rejecting all changes in the Church of Scotland since 1580.

For the following fifty years, the 'covenanters' faced considerable persecution. The Glorious Revolution of 1688, however, saw the ousting of the Roman Catholic King James VII (II of England) and his replacement by the Protestant King William II (III of England) and Queen Mary II , bringing religious toleration.

The Church of Scotland once again became Presbyterian in 1690, leading to the formation of the Scottish Episcopal Church by those Scots who wanted to continue worshipping within the Anglican Church. At the same time, the Reformed Presbyterian Church of Scotland was established by former covenanters who didn't wish to be part of the Church of Scotland. They were also known as the 'Cameronians'.

9.1 The Church of Scotland
At parish level, the Church operates through the kirk session, consisting of the minister and the principal members of the congregation, known as 'elders'. Above the kirk session, at district level, are the presbyteries and the national General Assembly. Until the early 1990s, at regional level there were also synods.

The Presbytery of Edinburgh (one of forty-six presbyteries in Scotland) covers roughly the same area as the City of Edinburgh unitary authority. The General Assembly meets annually in Edinburgh in May, when it elects a Moderator as leader of the Church for the following year. The first woman Moderator, Dr Alison Elliot, was elected in 2004.

For about 300 years before the introduction of civil registration in Scotland in 1855, the Church of Scotland recorded baptisms, marriages and burials within its parish registers, and it continues to do so. Although the instruction to begin recording these events was given in 1552, the earliest parish records existing from the fifteen parishes that now form the City of Edinburgh are the Canongate baptisms and marriages, dating from 1564, with burials from 1565.

For most of its history as a Protestant Church from 1560 onwards, the Church of Scotland had no bishops or archbishops. Even during the period when it did have them, no bishops' transcripts were produced from the Scottish parish registers.

In Scotland, there are also several other Presbyterian Churches, as well as the Roman Catholic Church and non-conformist churches such as the Scottish Episcopalian, Methodist and Baptist Churches. The Presbyterian Churches broke away from the Church of Scotland during the eighteenth and nineteenth centuries and are therefore also known as 'secession churches'.

Because many people were worshipping at other churches, and as a result of charges for recording baptisms, marriages and burials imposed at the end of the eighteenth century, many of these events were not recorded in Church of Scotland parish registers. This was not only the situation in remote country areas, but also in the major Scottish cities of Edinburgh and Glasgow.

Dr James Cleland, co-author of the Glasgow entry in the *New Statistical Account of Scotland* published in 1845, described this trend: 'While the great importance of accurate Parochial registers is admitted by all, it is astonishing how little they have been attended to in this country. In Edinburgh, the metropolis of Scotland, a city distinguished for its erudition, and for its numerous and valuable institutions, the baptismal register is miserably defective.'

Defective or not, the recently established General Register Office for Scotland (GROS) called in all the existing Church of Scotland parish registers up to the end of 1854. Known as the Old Parochial or Old Parish Registers (OPRs), they are held in Edinburgh at New Register House.

The following table shows the years covered by the registration of baptisms, marriages and burials in the fifteen parishes that are now included in the City of Edinburgh unitary authority area. The earliest year with register entries is shown, plus any large gaps in the registers. Unless indicated otherwise, the end year for the register entries is 1854.

Parish (NRS p. no.)	Baptisms	Marriages	Burials
Edinburgh (685/1)	1595	1595 (gap in 1695)	1820 (Buccleuch Ch.yd.)
St Cuthbert's (685/2)	1573 (gap 1643-1654)	1655	1740
Canongate (685/3)	1564 (gap 1568-1599)	1564 (gaps 1568-1599 and 1632-1644)	1565-1568
North Leith (692/1)	1615 (gap 1727)	1605 (gap 1707-1782)	1754
South Leith (692/2)	1599 (gap 1621-1642)	1588	1622-1819
Colinton (or Hailes) (677)	1654	1654	1716
Corstorphine (678)	1634	1665	1710
Cramond (679)	1651	1651	1816
Currie (682)	1638	1649	1662
Dalmeny (665)	1679	1628	1679-1816
Duddingston (684)	1631	1653 (gap 1818-1819)	1631
Kirkliston (667)	1675	1675	1817-1836
Liberton (693)	1624	1631	1647-1819
Queensferry (670)	1635	1635 (gap 1814-1819)	1782
Ratho (698a)	1682	1741	1682-1689

You won't find as much information in the parish register baptisms, marriages and burials as in civil registration births, marriages and deaths. The details you're likely to find in a baptism record are as follows:

Parish register baptism record, 1784. (Reproduced with the kind permission of the Registrar General for Scotland.)

Parish register marriage record, 1814. (Reproduced with the kind permission of the Registrar General for Scotland.)

- The child's name;
- The names of both parents, including the maiden name of the mother (although sometimes the mother's name is not given at all);
- The date of baptism (and sometimes also the date of birth);

- The father's occupation;
- The parents' address (sometimes this is fairly general);
- Whether or not the child was illegitimate (although this tends to be included in earlier records).

The name of the bride's father is often given in marriage entries, but rarely that of the father of the groom. Many entries in the marriage registers are actually records of the proclamation of banns announcing the couple's intention to marry, and it's not always clear whether or not they did.

A woman's husband may be mentioned in her burial record, and in the case of a child's record the father's name is usually given. The burial entry for a man, however, will usually give very little information that differentiates him from other similarly-named men.

There was considerable variation in the format of register entries from one parish to another, and the standardised pre-printed form registers introduced in England and Wales in 1754 for marriages, and 1813 for baptisms and burials were not used in Scotland.

Parish register burial record, 1791. (Reproduced with the kind permission of the Registrar General for Scotland.)

9.2 The Roman Catholic Church
Despite the domination of Presbyterian Protestantism for the greater part of the last 450 years, Roman Catholicism is today an important force once more, practised by 24 per cent of the Scottish Christian population. Much of this growth is due to nineteenth century migration from Ireland.

You can view images of Roman Catholic baptism, marriage, burial and other records in Scotland at the ScotlandsPeople Centre in

Edinburgh or online at the ScotlandsPeople website, www.scotlands people.gov.uk. The baptisms are from 1703-1992, the marriages from 1736-1934 and the burials from 1742-1955. The other Roman Catholic records (from 1742-1909) include lists of communicants, confessions, confirmations, seat rents, sick visits and *status animarum* ('state of the souls') lists.

9.3 The Scottish Episcopal Church (in the Anglican Communion)
After the 'Glorious Revolution' in 1688, the Scottish Episcopal Church was set up as a separate Scottish Church. From the official end of Roman Catholicism as the state religion in Scotland in 1560 up to 1688, the Episcopalians had been a faction within the Church of Scotland who opposed Presbyterianism and supported a Church with bishops and archbishops. The Church of Scotland was alternately Presbyterian and Episcopalian during the seventeenth century. Scottish Episcopalians subsequently suffered persecution in much of the eighteenth century, on account of their support for the Jacobite pretenders to the throne.

A list of the pre-1855 Scottish Episcopal Church registers can be found in *Sources for Scottish Genealogy and Family History* by D J Steel (Society of Genealogists, 1970), which has a good deal of useful information about Scottish parish registers and non-conformism in Scotland.

9.4 Non-conformist Churches from England and Wales
In 1652, the first Baptist congregation was established in Leith. As many members of the congregation were English soldiers, the Baptist denomination practically disappeared once the English Army was withdrawn from Scotland in 1659. A Baptist revival did take place a century later, however. Most counties had Baptist churches by 1835 and a Scotch Baptist Association was founded, later known as the Baptist Union of Scotland.

As early as 1653, a Society of Friends ('Quaker') meeting was founded in Lanarkshire. Persecution followed, however, and meetings were prohibited by the Scots Quaker Act of 1661. In spite of this, an Aberdeen Monthly Meeting began in 1672, and as part of the 1688 Revolution Settlement, the 1661 Act was rescinded. There was general toleration of Quakers after that (although mobs attacked them in both

Edinburgh and Glasgow in 1701, and the windows of the Edinburgh meeting-house were smashed in 1708), but the society never had much success in Scotland. You can find some information on Scottish Quakers in the Library at Friends House in London.

In the eighteenth century, Methodist Societies were founded in Dunbar, East Lothian in 1755, and in Edinburgh in 1764. Methodist circuits were established in Aberdeen, Glasgow, Edinburgh and Dundee in 1765, and in Dunbar in 1766, Inverness in 1779 and Ayr in 1786. Methodism cannot be said to have been very successful in Scotland, however. Its peak year in the nineteenth century was 1819, when there were almost 3,800 members, but numbers later rose in the twentieth century, partly due to English migration.

Congregationalism began even later in Scotland than Methodism. At the end of the eighteenth century and the beginning of the nineteenth, eighty-five Congregational churches were founded, fifty-five of which became the Congregational Union of Scotland in 1812. The Congregational Union then merged in 1897 with another non-conformist church, the Evangelical Union, which had been founded in 1843.

9.5 Presbyterian Secession Churches

As well as the non-conformist churches mentioned above, Scotland also had (and still has, to a certain extent) many Presbyterian Churches which broke away from the Church of Scotland. This movement away from the national Church began at the end of the seventeenth century and continued during the eighteenth, nineteenth and even twentieth centuries.

The first church to break away was the Original Secession Church, founded by the Revd Ebenezer Erskine and others in 1733, over the controversial system of 'patronage'. Erskine and his colleagues were opposed to landowners being able to appoint ministers to the churches on their estates. The Original Secession Church then split in 1747 into 'Burghers' (officially known as the Associate Synod) and 'Anti-Burghers' (the General Associate Synod). The division came about as a result of a divergence of opinion on the requirement for burgesses (city dignitaries) in Edinburgh, Glasgow and Perth to take an oath acknowledging 'the true religion'.

In 1761, the Revd Thomas Gillespie was expelled from the Church of Scotland over patronage, whereupon he and two colleagues founded the Relief Church (officially the Presbytery of Relief).

Next arose a dispute over whether the state should support the Church ('establishmentarianism') or whether they should be completely independent of one another ('disestablishmentarianism' or 'voluntaryism'). The establishmentarians were popularly known as 'Auld Lichts' (Old Lights), while the disestablishmentarians were called 'New Lichts' (New Lights). Both the Burghers and Anti-Burghers divided into Auld Lichts and New Lichts, the former in 1799 and the latter in 1806.

The biggest exit from the Church of Scotland took place in 1843, again over patronage, which was still a big issue, particularly in the Highlands. In that year, the Revd Thomas Chalmers and over 450 other ministers (about one third of the total number) left to form a new Free Church of Scotland. This, the largest of the secessions, was so big that it was known as the 'Disruption'. Eight years later, the Free Church's 450 congregations had doubled in number.

9.6 Reunification of the Secession Churches

After these secessions from the Church of Scotland came various unions of some of the secession churches with each other, as well as reunions with the Church of Scotland. At each union, however, some congregations always seemed to choose to remain independent. For example, in 1820, 154 of the 'New Licht' Burgher congregations joined 129 'New Licht' Anti-Burgher congregations under the name of the United Secession Church (or United Associate Synod of the Secession Church). Twenty years later, the 'Auld Licht' Burghers rejoined the Church of Scotland, although their Anti-Burgher counterparts remained as the Original Secession Church.

The 400 congregations of the United Secession Church (United Associate Congregations) formed in 1820 merged, in 1847, with 118 of the 136 congregations of the Relief Church, which had been founded in 1761. By 1851, the combined Church, known as the United Presbyterian Church, had 465 congregations.

In 1852, the Original Secession Church (the 'Auld Licht' Anti-Burghers) joined the Free Church, as did the Reformed Presbyterian Church in 1876. (The Reformed Presbyterian Church had been set up in 1690 by people who didn't want to be part of the Church of

Scotland.) In both cases, some congregations remained outside the mergers and formed 'continuing' Churches.

In 1893, the Free Presbyterian Church was formed by some members of the Free Church, but most of the main body of the Free Church merged with the United Presbyterian Church in 1900 as the United Free Church (after many years' negotiation). As usual, there were those in the Free Church who chose not to join the united Church (in this case, twenty-five ministers and sixty-three congregations – principally in the Highlands and Islands – known in Scotland as the 'wee frees'). In 1929, the United Free Church rejoined the Church of Scotland, although again a minority did not.

All these secessions and reunions may seem odd and far removed from modern times, and yet secessions still take place – in 1989, the Associated Presbyterian Churches broke away from the Free Presbyterian Church, and in 2000, the Free Church Continuing seceded from the Free Church.

The Presbyterian churches in Scotland today (and the approximate numbers of their congregations in Scotland) are the:

- Church of Scotland – with 1,118 congregations;
- Free Church of Scotland – with more than 100 congregations;
- United Free Church of Scotland – with about 65 congregations;
- Free Presbyterian Church of Scotland – with 34 congregations;
- Free Church of Scotland (Continuing) – with 29 congregations;
- Associated Presbyterian Churches – with 11 active congregations;
- Reformed Presbyterian Church of Scotland – with 6 congregations.

9.7 Where are the Church of Scotland records located?
The National Records of Scotland (NRS) holds the Church of Scotland parish registers and kirk session records. You can view the parish registers at the ScotlandsPeople Centre in Edinburgh (see Appendix 2) or online at the ScotlandsPeople website, www.scotlandspeople.gov.uk (see Appendix 1).

You can also search the LDS Church's indexes of the baptisms and marriages on the free Family Search site, www.familysearch.org, at Findmypast.co.uk, www.findmypast.co.uk, and at Ancestry.co.uk, www.ancestry.co.uk, (but beware the fact that a father's name in the marriage index will be displayed only in Ancestry's 'View Record' preview). You'll also find transcriptions of Scottish baptisms, marriages and burials at the FreeREG Project website, www.freereg.org.uk.

Some kirk session entries were entered in the parish registers, and correspondingly, some baptisms, marriages and burials were recorded in the kirk session registers. You can view digitised copies of the kirk session records as 'virtual volumes' at the NRS, as well as at many archives elsewhere in Scotland. Unfortunately, the digitised versions of the kirk session records have not yet been made available via the Internet.

9.8 Other Church records held by the NRS

Most of the records of the seceding Presbyterian Churches passed to the Church of Scotland in 1929 or earlier, and these were transferred to what is now the National Records of Scotland (NRS) in 1961. You'll find many of the records of the seceding churches under NRS collection reference CH3. These include registers of baptisms, marriages and burials, and minutes of the kirk sessions.

The NRS also has records of some 'Quaker' meetings (reference CH10), as well as of Methodist (CH11), Episcopal (CH12), United Free (CH13), Congregational (CH14), Unitarian (CH15), Free (CH16) and Roman Catholic congregations (RH21).

The following registers of seceding Presbyterian and non-conformist Churches within what is now the City of Edinburgh unitary authority are held by the NRS. The numbers in brackets are the Church of Scotland parish numbers. An asterisk shows that images of these records are available to view at the NRS on 'virtual volumes' (unfortunately not yet accessible online), while 'FS' indicates records indexed on FamilySearch.

Currie (682)
- Balerno United Associate Congregation (later UP, UF and CoS) – baptisms 1832-1836*; banns 1932-1977 (CH3/345).

Duddingston (684)
- Portobello, Bath Street/Windsor Place United Associate Congregation (later UP, UF and CoS) – baptisms 1836-1876*, 1875-1915*, 1924-1926*, 1927-1972; banns 1932-1958, 1960-1972 (CH3/933);
- Portobello, Regent Street United Presbyterian Church (later UF and

CoS) – baptisms 1879-1952* (CH3/934);
- Portobello, St Philip's Free Church (later UF and CoS) – banns 1959-1971 (CH3/957).

Edinburgh (685)
Presbyterian:
- Arthur Street Relief Church (later UP, UF, Pleasance UF and Pleasance CoS) – baptisms 1848-1859*, 1875-1917*, 1919-1953; banns 1932-1951 (CH3/432);
- Barclay Free Church (an offshoot of Fountainbridge Free Church in 1864; later UF and CoS) – baptisms 1862-1896 (CH3/1154);
- Bread Street United Presbyterian Church (later Viewforth UP and Bruntsfield UF) – baptisms 1829-1874, (1829-1860 on FS); (marriages 1844-1853 on FS, but not mentioned in NRS catalogue) (CH3/112);
- Bristo Associate Congregation (later UP, UF and CoS) – baptisms 1772-1783*, 1837-1936* (1680, 1773-1783 and 1837-1936 on FS) (CH3/313);
- Candlish Free Church, Merchiston (an offshoot of Fountainbridge United Free Church in 1901; later CoS) – baptisms 1882-1912*, 1913-1981 (CH3/959);
- Canongate United Presbyterian Church (later UF, Moray Knox UF and CoS) – baptisms 1883-1910* (CH3/582);
- Chalmers' Memorial Free Church (later Grange UF and CoS) – baptisms 1906-1968; marriages 1906-1944; banns 1932-1968 (CH3/715);
- Colinton and Currie Free Church (later Juniper Green Free Church, UF and Juniper Green St Andrew's CoS) – baptisms 1941-1973; banns 1932-1977 (CH3/951);
- Cowgate Free Church (later UF, Union UF and College CoS) – baptisms 1877-1910* (CH3/431);
- Cowgate United Associate Congregation (later Infirmary Street UP, Mayfield Secession Church UP, Fountainhall Road UF and CoS) – baptisms 1838-1843*, 1844-1855*; marriages 1844-1855* (CH3/1014);
- Dalry Free Church (later UF and CoS) – baptisms 1911-1960; banns 1932-1962 (CH3/616);
- Dean Free Church (later UF, St. Cuthbert's UF and Belford CoS) – baptisms 1845-1900* (1845-1881 on FS) (CH3/511);

- Fountainbridge Free Church (later UF, St George's Home Mission and Fountainbridge CoS) – baptisms 1923-1974; banns 1951-1973 (CH3/773);
- German Congregation Church – baptisms 1884-1914; confirmations 1885-1914; marriages 1885-1913; burials 1884-1914 (CH3/940);
- Gorgie Free Church (later UF and North Merchiston CoS) – baptisms 1899-1986; banns 1941-1977 (CH3/710);
- Guthrie Memorial Free Church (later UF and CoS) – baptisms 1894-1962*; banns 1932-1962 (CH3/747);
- Haymarket United Presbyterian Church (later UF and CoS) – baptisms 1872-1902*, 1902-1916, 1932-1959; banns 1935-1960 (CH3/615);
- High Free Church (later UF and Reid Memorial CoS) – baptisms 1864-1896 (CH3/967);
- James Place Relief Church (later UP, St James's Place UF and CoS, and Barony/St James's Place CoS) – baptisms 1799-1822*, 1816-1843*, 1844-1921*; banns 1932, 1932-1950, 1950-1956 (CH3/722);
- Lady Glenorchy's Free Church (later UF, Lady Glenorchy's North CoS and Hillside CoS) – baptisms 1903-1956; banns 1932-1952 (CH3/723);
- Lothian Road United Associate Congregation (formerly Gardner's Crescent UA, later UP, UF and CoS) – baptisms 1831-1875* (1820-1870 on FS) (CH3/417);
- Martyrs' Reformed Presbyterian Church (later Free Church and UF) – baptisms 1805-1896; marriages 1805-1896; deaths 1805-1846 (CH3/1198);
- Merchiston United Presbyterian Church (later John Ker Memorial UF and CoS) – baptisms 1912-1981; banns 1932-1952, 1952-1971, 1971-1977 (CH3/1254);
- Moray Free Church (later UF, Moray Knox UF and Moray Knox CoS) – baptisms 1875-1910* (CH3/583);
- Newhaven Free Church (later UF and Newhaven St Andrew's CoS) – baptisms 1857-1893*, 1917-1932; marriages 1857-1893*, 1917-1932; banns 1958-1974; burials 1917-1932 (CH3/824);
- Newington Free Church (later UF and Newington East CoS) – baptisms 1885-1931*; banns 1932-1942 (CH3/1195);
- New North Free Church (later UF and CoS) – baptisms 1852-1939* (CH3/468);

- Nicholson Street General Associate (Antiburgher) Congregation (later UP, UF and CoS) – baptisms 1831-1856*, 1896-1926*, 1940-1969; banns 1932-1969 (CH3/617);
- North Richmond Street United Presbyterian Church (later UF, CoS and Richmond Craigmillar CoS) – baptisms 1861-1902*, 1911-1930; banns 1932-1944, 1945-1950, 1950-1959, 1959-1969, 1969-1977 (CH3/576);
- Pleasance Free Church (later UF and Union UF) – baptisms 1878-1908* (CH3/639);
- Portsburgh Associate Congregation (later UP, Lauriston Place UF and Lauriston CoS) – baptisms 1866-1889*, 1890-1957* (CH3/1152);
- Potterrow United Presbyterian Church (later Hope Park UP, UF and CoS) – baptisms 1790-1857, 1790-1825*, 1826-1857* (1793-1825, 1825-1862 on FS); (marriages 1801-1865 and 1825-1862 on FS, but not mentioned in NRS catalogue) (CH3/112);
- Restalrig Free Church (later UF and New Restalrig CoS) – banns 1932-1944, 1944-1959, 1969-1980 (CH3/714);
- Rose Street United Associate Church (later UP, Palmerston Place UF and CoS) – baptisms 1854-1928*; baptismal fees January-June 1836* (CH3/950);
- Roseburn Free Church (later UF and CoS) – baptisms 1873-1962*; banns 1932-1962 (CH3/521);
- Roxburgh Free Church (later Roxburgh-McCrie Free Church, UF, Newington UF and Newington East CoS) – baptisms 1880-1920* (CH3/1194);
- St Andrew's Free Church (later UF and St Andrew's Drumsheugh CoS) – baptisms 1884-1954*; banns 1932-1955 (CH3/118);
- St Columba's Gaelic Free Church (later St Columba's Free Church, UF, CoS and Highland Church CoS) – baptisms 1852-1855*; banns 1934-1952 (CH3/709);
- St Cuthbert's Free Church (later UF and Belford CoS) – baptisms 1872-1911*, 1911-1969; marriages 1898-1912* (CH3/510);
- St David's Free Church (later UF and St David's, Morrison Street, CoS) – baptisms 1863-1961*; banns 1932-1955, 1956-1961; (marriages 1844 on FS, but not mentioned in NRS catalogue) (CH3/113);
- St George's Free Church (later UF and St George's West CoS) – baptisms 1845-1854*; banns 1932-1946, 1946-1958, 1958-1969, 1969-1977 (CH3/965);

- St Luke's Free Church (later Queen Street UF and CoS) – baptisms 1843-1947* (CH3/782);
- St Mary's Free Church (later UF, Barony CoS and Barony/St James's Place CoS) – baptisms 1873-1878*, 1901-1957 (CH3/721);
- St Paul's Free Church (later UF, CoS and St Paul's Newington CoS) – baptisms 1876-1941*, 1930-1984; banns 1945-1955, 1955-1965, 1965-1983 (CH3/455);
- Slateford United Associate Congregation (later UP, UF and CoS) – banns 1935-1954 (CH3/490);
- South College Street Relief Church (later College UP, College UF, Union UF and College CoS) – baptisms 1766-1783* (CH3/433);
- Stockbridge Free Church (later UF and CoS) – baptisms 1880-1904*, 1910-1975; banns 1956-1975 (CH3/702);
- Viewforth Free Church (an offshoot of Fountainbridge Free Church in 1872; later UF and CoS) – baptisms 1875-1960*; banns 1948-1962 (CH3/1029);
- Warrender Park Free Church (later UF and Warrender CoS) – baptisms 1900-1972; banns 1951-1972 (CH3/739);
- West Port Free Church (later Chalmers' Territorial UF and Chalmers CoS) – baptisms 1845-1878* (CH3/1153).

Methodist
- Edinburgh Mission Primitive Methodist Church – baptisms 1833-1838, 1843-1844 (CH1/16);
- Edinburgh Wesleyan Methodist Circuit – baptisms 1811-1818 (CH11/1);
- Nicolson Square Wesleyan Methodist Church – baptisms 1801-1871(CH1/2).

Episcopal
- St Columba's-by-the-Castle Episcopal Church – baptisms 1842-1882 (includes St Paul's Carrubber's Close 1842-1846, from which St Columba's had broken away), 1882-1887, 1887-1894, 1883-1891 (house of charity), 1894-2003; confirmations 1847-1871, 1889-1929; marriages 1846-1849, 1850-1886, 1886-1887, 1887-1894, 1894-1909, 1909-1957; burials 1874-1925 (CH12/5);
- St John the Evangelist's Episcopal Church (formerly Charlotte Chapel) – baptisms 1797-1851*, 1852-1892, 1873-1920; confirmations 1873-1918, 1920-1941; marriages 1813-1852*, 1852-

1872, 1873-1934; burials 1813-1851*, 1829-1853, 1904-1969 (CH12/3);
- St Kentigern's Episcopal Church – baptisms 1873-1904, 1904-1941; confirmations 1874-1928; marriages 1873-1926, 1926-1941; burials 1873-1926 (CH12/4).

Unitarian
- St Mark's Unitarian Church – baptisms 1841-1853, 1854-1971; marriages 1854-1971; deaths 1854-1971 (CH15/1).

Free Church
- Greyfriars Free Church (later Buccleuch-Greyfriars Free Church) – baptisms 1844-1885 (CH16/2).

Religious Society of Friends (Quakers)
- South East Scotland Monthly Meeting – births 1664-1748, 1670-1787 (with gaps), 1763, 1787-1793, 1787-1794, 1795-1870, 1798-1803, 1828-1835, 1835-1840, 1840-1850, 1852-1856, 1857-1874, 1863, 1872-1880, 1878-1884, 1884-1901, 1901-1909, 1908-1918, 1918-1949, 1950-1959; marriages 1659-1720, 1786-1790, 1786-1793, 1796-1950; deaths 1668-1727, 1798, 1807; burials 1680-1716, 1788-1789, 1788-1793, 1791-1795, 1795-1921, 1828-1838, 1839-1847, 1857-1861, 1863-1880, 1881-1890, 1890-1904, 1904-1909, 1910-1914, 1915-1919, 1920-1928, 1928-1935, 1935-1941, 1941-1948, 1948-1961 (CH10/1);
- Quarterly Meeting of North Britain – births 1796-1861; Burials 1796-1878, 1797-1860 (also CH10/1).

Kirkliston (667)
- Kirkliston Free Church (later UF and Newliston CoS) – baptisms 1843-1943*; marriages 1844-1852*, 1904*, 1929-1930* (CH3/1008).

Leith (692)
Presbyterian
- St John's (West) Free Church (later UF and CoS) – baptisms 1846-1874* (CH3/211);
- Leith, North Free Church (later UF and CoS) – banns 1902-1977, 1933-1949, 1949-1961 (CH3/339);

- Leith, North/Coburg/Harper Memorial Associate Congregation (later UA, UP, UF and CoS) – banns 1932-1940 (CH3/447);
- Leith Mariners' Free Church (later UF and CoS) – baptisms 1841-1881*, 1882-1961*, (1841-1873 on FS); marriages 1842-1858*; banns 1932-1961 (CH3/448);
- Kirkgate General Associate (Antiburgher) Congregation (later Burgher, UP, UF and CoS) – baptisms 1800-1815*, 1933-1973; banns 1932-1973 (CH3/495);
- Junction Road Relief Church (later UP, UF and CoS) – baptisms 1825-1858*, 1832-1854*, 1856-1867*, 1865-1879*, 1879-1975*; marriages 1837-1855*, 1856-1869*; banns 1932-1946, 1947-1968, 1968-1973 (CH3/728);
- Bonnington United Presbyterian Church (later UF and CoS) – baptisms 1877-1967*; banns 1932-1967 (CH3/743);
- Leith, South Free Church (later UF and Claremont CoS) – baptisms 1898-1973; banns 1932-1949, 1950-1959, 1959-1969, 1969-1977 (CH3/825);
- St Andrew's Place General Associate (Antiburgher) Congregation (later UP, UF and CoS) – baptisms 1789*, 1794-1882*, 1882-1973*; marriages 1795-1872*; banns 1932-1965 (CH3/826).

Methodist
- St Clair Street Methodist Church – baptisms 1833-1921, 1918-1963, 1966 (CH11/7);
- Great Junction Street Wesleyan Church – baptisms 1834-1875, 1891-1924, 1925-1933, 1933-1972; baptismal certificates 1919-1920, 1953-1954, 1969-1975; marriages 1933-1972 (CH11/12).

Episcopal
- St James's Episcopal Church – baptisms 1733-1761, 1735-1775, 1809-1846, 1847-1863, 1863-1872, 1872-1881, 1881-1896, 1896-1919, (1733-1775 on FS); confirmations 1736-1769, 1852-1863, 1864-1884, 1885-1903; marriages 1738-1775, 1813-1836, 1836-1863, 1863-1874, 1875-1885, 1885-1910, 1910-1965, (1738-1775 on FS); burials 1828-1850, 1863-1875, 1875-1895, 1895-1924, 1925-1968 (CH12/1).

Queensferry (670)
- Queensferry Associate Congregation (later UAS, UP, South

Queensferry UF and South Queensferry St Andrew's CoS) –
baptisms 1855-1956*; banns 1932-1955 (CH3/621).

Ratho (698)

- Ratho and Kirknewton Free Church (later UF and Wilkieston CoS)
  – baptisms 1886-1961*, 1962-1968; banns 1933-1968 (CH3/268).

Although, at the time of publication, the records of the above churches
have not been digitised and made available on the ScotlandsPeople
website, some of the records have been indexed in the 'Scotland, Births
and Baptisms' and 'Scotland, Marriages' databases located on the LDS
Church's FamilySearch site, https://familysearch. org.

Information on which churches are in these databases is available
on Steve Archer's website 'FamilySearch: a Guide to the British
batches', at www.archersoftware.co.uk/igi/index.htm. You can also find
this on Hugh Wallis's IGI Batch Numbers site, http://tinyurl.
com/HughWallisIGI.

Chapter 10

DEATH IN EDINBURGH

In Scotland there are three types of burial grounds – parish churchyards, local authority burial grounds and privately-run cemeteries – all of which are found in Edinburgh. Prior to the introduction of burial grounds run by local authorities through the Burial Grounds (Scotland) Act of 1855, most burials took place in parish churchyards (see below).

10.1 Cemeteries and crematoria

In the 1840s, however, six privately-owned cemeteries were opened in areas then on the outskirts of Edinburgh: Warriston (in 1843), Dean (1845), Dalry (1846), Rosebank (1846) Echobank, later renamed Newington (1846) and Grange (1847).

More private cemeteries were opened in the late nineteenth and early twentieth centuries: Morningside (1878), New Dalry, later renamed North Merchiston (1881), Eastern, in Drum Terrace, off Easter Road (1883), Piershill (1887), Seafield (1888), Mount Vernon, owned by the Roman Catholic Church (1895), Comely Bank (1898), Saughton (1919) and Corstorphine Hill (1930). Several of the private cemeteries were later extended.

Edinburgh Corporation took over fifteen churchyards in 1925 and also ran three cemeteries: Portobello, taken over when this area became part of Edinburgh in 1896, extended in 1931 and again in 1960; Liberton, as an extension to the churchyard in 1926, and later extended; and Mortonhall, opened in 1960.

The first privately-operated crematorium was opened in Edinburgh in 1929 at Warriston (the first in Scotland had been opened in Glasgow in 1895), which added a second, smaller chapel in 1957. Leith Crematorium (also privately run) was opened at Seafield in 1939.

At Mortonhall in 1967, Edinburgh Council opened a crematorium designed by Sir Basil Spence, the Bombay-born Scottish architect whose design for a new Coventry Cathedral won a competition to replace its bomb-damaged predecessor.

10.2 Obtaining more information on your ancestor's burial or cremation

The City of Edinburgh Council is now responsible for thirty-nine cemeteries and churchyards, including the historic churchyards of St Cuthbert's, Greyfriars, Canongate, Old Calton, New Calton, North Leith, South Leith and Restalrig. You can see the full list at www.edinburgh.gov.uk/directory/40/cemeteries_and_crematoria.

You can request information on burial records from Edinburgh Council's Bereavement Services, based at Mortonhall Crematorium, by emailing mortonhallcrematorium@edinburgh.gov.uk with the name of the deceased person, the exact date of his or her death, and last address (if known). There is a search charge of £16 per hour, which covers searches for up to four people.

The Edinburgh Eastern Cemetery Company Ltd, www.edinburgh cemeteries.co.uk, which operates the Eastern and Piershill cemeteries, holds its burial records on microfiche, which it will search for you. It is essential to provide the date of death, as the company's records are arranged chronologically.

Warriston and Seafield Crematoria have Online Books of Remembrance, at www.remembrance-books.com/warriston, and at www.remembrance-books.com/seafield respectively.

The pay-per-view and subscription website Deceased Online, www.deceasedonline.com, holds records of: more than 220,000 cremations that took place at Warriston from 1929-2009; nearly 50,000 cremations at Seafield from 1939-2009; and nearly 40,000 burials at Seafield from 1888-2011.

In addition, Deceased Online has photographs and transcripts of the memorial and headstone inscriptions from: Canongate Churchyard (1566-2003); Old Calton Burial Ground (1718-1948); New Calton Burial Ground (1742-2007); Dalmeny Churchyard (1601-1988); Kirkliston Churchyard and Cemetery (1526-2008); South Queensferry Old Church (1640-1962); and South Queensferry Cemetery (1871-2009).

You can also buy collections of the photographs and transcriptions of the memorial and headstone inscriptions in the above churchyards and cemeteries from the Scottish Monumental Inscriptions website, www.scottish-monumental-inscriptions.com. The collections are available either on CD or as digital downloads (text only).

As well as covering the above churchyards, the CDs and digital downloads are available for the following places: Colinton, St Cuthbert's Churchyard (1498-2011); Colinton Cemetery (1881-2012); Currie Churchyard and Cemetery (1675-2012); and Ratho Churchyard (1679-2001).

The Gravestone Photographic Resource, www.gravestonephotos. com, has images (taken by volunteers) and transcriptions of gravestones in: Greyfriars Churchyard; Canongate Churchyard; Dean Cemetery; Old Calton Burial Ground; New Calton Burial Ground; St John's Episcopal Churchyard and St Cuthbert's Churchyard (together); Cramond Churchyard; Gogar Churchyard; and part of Warriston Cemetery. You can request an image of a gravestone free of charge through the website.

The Find a Grave website, www.findagrave.com, has transcriptions of some of the memorials on the gravestones (and photographs of some of the stones) in many of Edinburgh's cemeteries and churchyards, including: Canongate Churchyard; Greyfriars Churchyard; St Cuthbert's Churchyard; Old Calton Burial Ground; New Calton Burial Ground; Corstorphine Hill; Dean; Eastern; Grange; Liberton; Mount Vernon; Newington (Echobank); Piershill; Rosebank; Saughton; Seafield (wrongly identified as being in West Lothian); Warriston; North Leith; and South Leith. Many of the burials transcribed are those of servicemen.

Transcriptions of the burials in Greyfriars Churchyard and at the Chapel Royal, Holyrood are also accessible at the FreeREG website, www.freereg.org.uk.

(See also Appendix A3.1 for the Scottish Genealogy Society's 'Black Book', which has details of its holdings of death and burial records, and monumental inscriptions.)

10.3 St Cuthbert's Churchyard
St Cuthbert's Church (also known as the West Kirk) dates back to the eighth century and is believed to be the oldest of Edinburgh's churches, although until 1832, St Cuthbert's parish lay outside the royal burgh.

Among the few tombs inside the church is that of the mathematician John Napier, the inventor of logarithms, who was born in 1550 and died in 1617. Napier lived in Merchiston Castle (see Appendix 5), which is now part of Edinburgh Napier University (see Chapter 16).

The oldest gravestone in St Cuthbert's Churchyard is that of Henry Nisbet of Dean, who died in 1692. James Donaldson, a printer, who was buried there in 1830, left £200,000 for the founding of Donaldson's Hospital, which was completed in 1850 (see Chapter 15).

Thomas de Quincy, born in Manchester in 1786 and the author of *The Confessions of an Opium Eater*, was buried in the churchyard in 1859. Also there lies George Meikle Kemp, architect of the Scott Monument, who died in 1844 after falling into the Union Canal on his way to meet boats carrying cargoes of stones for the monument.

'Body-snatchers' (such as the infamous Burke and Hare) were active in Edinburgh in the early nineteenth century. To deter them, St Cuthbert's Church authorities placed heavy gratings over new graves and stationed armed night-watchmen in guardhouses.

In 1841, graves in a new southern section of the churchyard (opened in 1834) had to be moved to allow the construction of a railway tunnel for the Edinburgh and Glasgow Railway Company.

In 1864, at the instigation of the newly appointed Medical Officer of Health, Henry Littlejohn, several burial grounds in the city were closed. St Cuthbert's Church resisted closing the common areas of its main churchyard, as well as its extensions in Buccleuch Street and East Preston Street, and so these were not closed until 1874, after a year-long inquiry.

10.4 St Giles' Churchyard

St Giles' Cathedral (also known as the High Kirk of Edinburgh) is the oldest church that lies within the old boundary of the royal burgh, dating back to the ninth century.

The churchyard lay between the south side of the church and the Cowgate, but had become so overcrowded that it was closed in 1566, when Mary, Queen of Scots gave Edinburgh the gardens of the Greyfriars' Monastery for use as a burial ground. John Knox was buried in St Giles' Churchyard in 1572, although it was officially closed at the time.

Unfortunately, there is no sign of the churchyard today, as it has all been covered over, either by buildings or roadways. Work began in 1632 on the construction of the Parliament Hall and the Court of Session in

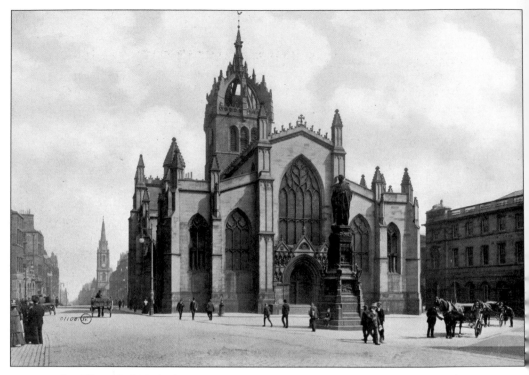

St Giles' Cathedral, late nineteenth century. From Edinburgh and its Environs (Valentine & Sons, c.1901).

what became Parliament Square; houses on the east side later became the Police Chambers. The Signet Library was built to the west, and coffins and human remains were still being found when the building was altered in 1844.

In 1879, 'several tons of bones' (according to the *Third Statistical Account of Scotland*) that had been buried under the floor in St Giles' Church itself were removed and reburied in Greyfriars Churchyard.

10.5 Greyfriars Churchyard
In 1224, Agnellus of Pisa and eight Franciscan brothers arrived in England. Known as the Greyfriars, they established communities in Britain and Ireland, and built a monastery in Edinburgh early in the fifteenth century. When Scotland became Protestant in 1560 the monastery was attacked and left in ruins, and the friars fled to the Netherlands.

As mentioned above, the churchyard was opened as a burial-place in 1566, and the first burials took place in 1568, a plague year in

Edinburgh. One of the earliest monuments within the churchyard was dedicated to George Heriot, goldsmith, the father of the founder of George Heriot's School (see Chapter 15), who died in 1610.

Other notable people buried there include:

- James Douglas, 4th Earl of Morton and Regent of Scotland (who was executed in 1581 for his supposed part in the murder of Darnley – see Appendix A6.1 – and whose head was buried at Greyfriars in 1582);
- Sir George Mackenzie of Rosehaugh, who prosecuted Covenanters, was nick-named 'Bluidy Mackenzie, died in London in 1691, and is said to haunt his mausoleum in the churchyard;
- Allan Ramsay (1686-1758), the poet, who established the first circulating library in Scotland;
- James Craig (1739-1795), architect, who won a competition to design Edinburgh's New Town (see Chapter 3);
- Mary Erskine (1629-1707), born in Clackmannanshire, who set up a private bank and was the benefactor of the school renamed in her honour (see Chapter 15);
- George Watson (1654-1723), chief accountant of the Bank of Scotland, who bequeathed money to endow the school named after him (see Chapter 15);
- William Creech (1745-1815), publisher of the first Edinburgh edition of Robert Burns' poems and of the *Statistical Account of Scotland* (see Chapter 19), and Lord Provost of Edinburgh 1811-1813;
- John Porteous, Captain of Edinburgh's City Guard, who was lynched there by a mob in 1736;
- William McGonagall (1825-1902), 'poet and tragedian', author of many poems considered to be doggerel.

Also buried at Greyfriars are about 100 Covenanters, who were executed between 1661 and 1688 and commemorated by a Martyrs' Monument erected in 1706. In addition, forty-one Lord Provosts, thirty-six Lords of Session and Lord Advocates, and thirty Principals and Professors of Edinburgh University are buried there.

The Skye terrier known as 'Greyfriars Bobby', who is said to have remained by his late master John Gray's grave for fourteen years, and who died in 1872, aged sixteen, is also buried at Greyfriars in an unconsecrated area of the churchyard.

The churchyard was closed in the 1860s, except to owners of private tombs.

10.6 St John's Episcopal Churchyard

Construction of the Church of St John the Evangelist began in 1816, to house the Anglican congregation founded by the Reverend Daniel Sandford, born near Dublin in 1766. Sandford became Bishop of Edinburgh in the Scottish Episcopal Communion, was the incumbent of St John's Church for the twelve years following its dedication in 1818, and was buried in the churchyard in 1830.

Sir Henry Raeburn (1756-1823), the famous painter, is buried in this churchyard, as are several professors at the University of Edinburgh (see Chapter 16). These include Dr William Pulteney Alison (Medicine), born in Edinburgh in 1790, died in 1855; Sir William Hamilton, 1788-1856 (Universal History, and then Logic), born in Glasgow; and Macvey Napier, 1777-1847 (Conveyancing), born in Kirkintilloch. Napier edited a six-volume supplement to the *Encyclopædia Britannica* in 1824 and also edited the *Edinburgh Review* for seventeen years from 1829.

Also buried in St John's Churchyard are George Moir (Rhetoric, and then Scots Law), born in Aberdeen, died in 1870; and James Syme (Clinical Surgery, both at the University of Edinburgh and at University College London), born in Kinross-shire, Surgeon to the Queen for Scotland, died in 1870.

Burials took place in St John's Churchyard from 1818 up to 1965. You can take a virtual tour of the churchyard (known as the 'Peace Garden') on the church's website: www.stjohns-edinburgh.org.uk/visit-st-john-s/peace_garden.html.

10.7 Canongate Churchyard

Canongate Church was built in 1688, as King James VII (II of England) had turned Holyrood Abbey Church, where the inhabitants of the burgh of Canongate had worshipped since the Reformation, into a Roman Catholic chapel.

In Canongate Churchyard Robert Fergusson, the poet (1750-1774) is buried, whose interment in a pauper's grave is marked by a simple stone erected by Robert Burns thirteen years later.

More successful in life and better remembered are Dr Adam Smith (1723-1790), born in Kirkcaldy, who studied at the University of Glasgow and Balliol College Oxford. Professor of Logic and later Moral Philosophy at Glasgow University, before becoming Rector there, Smith was the author of an *Inquiry into the Wealth of Nations*.

Also buried in Canongate Churchyard are Dugald Stewart (1753-1828), Professor of Mathematics and later Moral Philosophy; Sir William Fettes, twice Lord Provost of Edinburgh, and founder of Fettes College (see Chapter 15), who died in 1836; and John Ballantyne (1774-1821), born in Kelso, publisher and friend of Sir Walter Scott.

A monument was erected in 1880 to the soldiers who died in Edinburgh Castle from 1692-1880, as the castle came under the ecclesiastical remit of the parish of Canongate. The churchyard was officially closed to new burials in the 1860s.

10.8 Old Calton Burial Ground

The burial ground was opened on the south side of the Calton Hill in 1718. Up to that time, the inhabitants of the burgh of Calton – which was part of the parish of South Leith – had been buried in South Leith Churchyard, in spite of it being about 2 miles distant.

The burial ground was cut through by the new street named Waterloo Place, and when this was constructed between 1815 and 1819, many of the gravestones and human remains were moved to the New Calton Burial Ground, nearly half a mile away.

Among the many distinguished people buried in the Old Calton Burial Ground are David Hume (1711-1776), philosopher and historian, and author of *A Treatise on Human Nature*, *Political Discourses* and *The History of England*; and Archibald Constable (1773-1827). Born in the parish of Carnbee in Fife, Constable became a bookseller and publisher, founding the *Farmer's Magazine* and the *Edinburgh Review*. He later became proprietor of the *Scots Magazine* and the *Encyclopædia Britannica*, but ended his life insolvent, with debts of over £250,000 in 1826.

Also interred in the Old Calton Burial Ground are William Blackwood (1776-1834), bookseller and publisher of *Blackwood's Magazine*; and Thomas Hamilton (1784-1858), who was born in Glasgow. Hamilton was the architect of the following Edinburgh buildings: the old Royal High School building on the south side of Calton Hill (see Chapter 15);

the Burns Monument; the Dean Orphanage; the Physicians' Hall; and the rebuilt St Mary's Church in South Leith.

A Martyrs' Monument designed by Thomas Hamilton was erected in the Old Calton Burial Ground in 1844, 'to the memory of James Muir, Thomas Tyshe Palmer, William Skirving, Maurice Margarot and Joseph Gerald'. In 1793 and 1794, these five men were transported to Australia for fourteen years for advocating that everyone, not just landowners, should have the right to vote. They were pardoned in 1838.

Also in the burial ground is the Scottish-American Soldiers' Monument, erected in 1893 to commemorate the five (now six) Scotsmen who volunteered in the army of the United States during the American Civil War: Sergeant Major John McEwan; Lieutenant Colonel William L Duff; Robert Steedman; James Wilkie; Robert Ferguson; and Alexander Smith (whose name was added in 1993).

New burials ceased in the Old Calton Burial Ground in 1869.

10.9 New Calton Burial Ground

Opened in 1817 as an extension to the Old Calton Burial Ground, the new burial ground was used for the re-interment of the remains found on the site of Waterloo Place. In New Calton lies the body of David Allan (1744-1796), artist and Director of the Academy of Art in Edinburgh, born in Alloa.

Other notable people interred in New Calton include the 'Lighthouse Stevensons', relatives of the author Robert Louis Stevenson (RLS): Robert Stevenson (1772-1850, RLS's grandfather), Superintendent of Northern Lighthouses, born in Glasgow; Thomas Stevenson (1818-1887, father of RLS), lighthouse designer and meteorologist; and Alan Stevenson (1807-1865, uncle of RLS), Engineer to the Board of Northern Lighthouses.

Also buried there is William Dick (1793-1866), Professor of Veterinary Surgery and founder of the Edinburgh Veterinary College (later renamed the Royal (Dick) Veterinary College – the 'Dick Vet' – and now a faculty of the University of Edinburgh).

Six admirals were also laid to rest in the New Calton Burial Ground: Rear Admiral James Bissett (died 1824); Vice Admiral Andrew Frazer (1747-1829); Rear Admiral Andrew Smith (died 1831); Admiral John Graham (1791-1854); Vice Admiral Thomas Frazer (1796-1870); and Admiral Peat (died 1879).

The New Calton Burial Ground was closed to new burials in the 1860s.

10.10 Holyrood Abbey burials

The abbey was founded in 1128 by King David I and served by a community of Augustinian Canons Regular, who had come from Merton Priory in Greater London. The abbey was damaged by the English Army under the Earl of Hertford (later Duke of Somerset) in 1544 and 1547, and by the Edinburgh mob in 1559.

King James VII (II of England) rebuilt the abbey as a Chapel Royal in 1687, but this was destroyed in the Glorious Revolution of 1688 by a mob, who also desecrated the tombs in the Royal Vault. Royalty buried within the vault include: David II (who died in 1371); James II (1460); his queen, Mary of Gueldres (who died in 1463, and whose remains were moved to Holyrood in 1848 from her Church of the Holy Trinity, which was removed – together with its burial ground – to make way for the Waverley Station and the new railway lines); James V (1542), his first queen Madeleine (1537); Henry Lord Darnley (1567); and ten infant princes and princesses.

Also buried in the abbey is Sir John Sinclair of Ulbster, who instigated and compiled the first *Statistical Account of Scotland* (see Chapter 19) and who died in 1835.

10.11 War memorials

After years of opposition to its creation, the Scottish National War Memorial (SNWM) was opened in 1927 in Crown Square within Edinburgh Castle. Inside the memorial building are rolls of honour naming over 100,000 Scottish servicemen and -women who were killed during the First World War. An additional 50,000 names were added after the Second World War, and names have been added more recently for soldiers killed in Iraq and Afghanistan. You can make a virtual tour of the memorial and search of the rolls of honour at the SNWM website, www.snwm.org.

Photographs of the war memorials at Seafield Cemetery and Crematorium are accessible online, at www.edinburghcrematorium. com/seafield_war_memorials.html. There are communal memorials for those who died in the First and Second World Wars, as well as a large number of individual soldiers' memorials.

Chapter 11

EDINBURGH WILLS AND INVENTORIES

11.1 Wills

Wills are very helpful for finding out more about your Edinburgh ancestors. Although by no means everybody made a will in the past, if members of your family did then their wills may well contain information you'd be very unlikely to come across elsewhere, and may enable you to confirm or determine family relationships.

Unlike in England and Wales, where wills are 'proved', in Scotland they are 'confirmed'. Strictly speaking, the documents are testaments, but they're generally known as wills. There are two types of testament: a testament testamentar (like an English will) and a testament dative (similar to an English administration). A relative or creditor may apply to the court for a testament dative, if a deceased person has left no will.

The Scottish courts responsible for dealing with testamentary matters were the commissary courts from the mid-sixteenth century up to the early nineteenth century. The commissary courts were then abolished and the commissary function passed to the existing sheriff courts, which deal with both civil and criminal cases. A commissary court's area of jurisdiction was called a commissariot and its boundaries were similar to those of the ancient Scottish dioceses.

The Edinburgh Commissary Court, which was founded in 1564 and closed in 1836, handled the confirmation of wills, not only of people who had lived in the Lothians but also of those who had died elsewhere in Scotland or overseas.

All Scottish wills and inventories from 1514 to a rolling cut-off point of ten years ago are held by the National Records of Scotland (NRS) in Edinburgh. More recent records are held by the Commissary Department of Edinburgh Sheriff Court (27 Chambers Street, Edinburgh EH1 1LB). At the NRS, wills and inventories can be viewed

Testament dative, 1891. (Crown Copyright, National Records of Scotland, SC70/1/299.)

free of charge. Via the ScotlandsPeople website, www.scotlandspeople.
gov.uk, you can search the index of wills and inventories up to 1925 free
of charge. To view and download a will or inventory costs ten credits,
whatever its length – and some can be more than forty pages long.

Both testaments testamentar and testaments dative usually include
an inventory of the moveable property of the deceased person. As will
be seen from the example discussed later in this chapter, an inventory
could be extremely detailed, listing all the items in the deceased
person's house, including all their clothes, books and even the bottles
of beer and spirits in the cellar!

Under Scots Law, moveable property was divided into a third for the widow (known as the *jus relictae*), and a third (or half, if the wife of the deceased was already dead) to be divided equally between all the children of the deceased, both male and female (called the *legitim* or 'bairns' pairt'). The deceased was able to bequeath the remaining third to whoever he wished, and this was therefore known as the 'deid's pairt'.

Up to 1868 and the passage of the Heritable Jurisdictions Act, land and buildings couldn't be willed to anyone through a testament testamentar. Land and buildings were 'heritable property' and these passed to the eldest son automatically through the law of inheritance (see below). A testator could get round this prohibition by setting up a trust (usually called a 'trust disposition and settlement') during his lifetime, which would then be implemented after his death.

Below is a transcript of the will and inventory of my seven times great-uncle, William Ruthven, who was a writer (solicitor) in Edinburgh during the eighteenth century.

Transcript of the testament testamentar and inventory of William Ruthven, Reference CC8/8/119, Edinburgh Commissary Court, 1763
Introductory section

'The testament testamentar and inventory of the goods, gear, debts and sums of money which were pertaining, addebted and resting owing to umquhile [= the late] William Ruthven, writer in Edinburgh, at the time of his decease, who deceased upon the day of [The date has been left blank, but there is a record of the burial of William Ruthven in Canongate Churchyard on 31 January 1763, aged 70 years.]

'Made and given up by himself upon the 25th of January 1763, in so far as concerns the nomination of his sole executor and universal legatee, and now made and given up by **James Dallas** writer in Edinburgh. In so far as concerns the inventory foresaid of the said defunct [= deceased], his debts and sums of money after-written, which **James Dallas** he the said defunct did nominate and appoint to be his sole executor, universal legatee and intromitter [= manager] with his haill [= whole] movables and executry after his death, and that by his disposition and assignation containing the foresaid nomination bearing date the

25th and registered in the Borrow [= Burgh] Court books of Edinburgh upon the 31st of January 1763 years hereafter engrossed.'

Inventory
'Follows the inventory:
In the first [place], the said defunct had of cash lying by him at the time of his death £2 8/9 sterling;

'£9 12/3 sterling as the produce of his body cloaks, linens, books, etc. rouped [= auctioned] off shortly after his death;

'The defunct's silver watch valued at £1 10/-, all sterling money, extending the goods and gear [= moveable belongings] before-written in haill [= whole] to £13 11/- sterling, which in Scots money is £162 12/-;

'There was addebted and resting owing to the said defunct at the time of his decease aforesaid the sum of £8 12/3 sterling as the balance of an account due by **John Chalmers**, writer [= solicitor] in Edinburgh, to the defunct for certain fees of Extracts of Decreets [= court judgements] and other affairs betwixt the said defunct and him including a debt of £5 sterling due by bill by the said **John Chalmers** to the defunct and interest due thereon as the said account docketed and signed by the said **John Chalmers** and **James Dallas** of date the 22nd of March 1763;

'The sum of 17/11 sterling as the defunct's fees due to him for record copies of Extracts, etc. from the 12th of March 1762 to January 1763, all sterling money, extending the said two sums to £9 10/2 sterling, which in Scots money is £114 2/-.'

This is a pretty basic inventory: apart from William Ruthven's silver watch, all his other personal belongings are covered by 'his body cloaks, linens, books, etc'. For a much more detailed example, see below for the inventory of William Ruthven's son, also named William.

The actual will
'Follows the defunct's disposition and assignation containing his foresaid nomination:
'I, **William Ruthven**, writer in Edinburgh, being resolved to settle my affairs and effects which shall belong to me at my death

to a trustee for payment of my debts so far as my said funds shall extend and in case of any reversions, that the same may go to **Thomas Ruthven**, wigmaker in London; **David**, **Elizabeth** and **Margaret Ruthven**, children of **David Ruthven**, my elder brother; and **Thomas Ruthven**, writer in Edinburgh, my nephews and nieces in the respective proportions after-mentioned, after payment of all charges and expenses attending the management of the said trust and a gratification to the said trustee,

'And having confidence in the fidelity and capacity of **James Dallas**, writer in Edinburgh, for executing the said trust, have therefore disponed [= bequeathed] and assigned like as I do hereby dispone and assign to and in favour of the said **James Dallas**, in case he survives me, in trust for the uses and purposes and with and under the express conditions, provisions, declarations and reservations after-mentioned:

'All and whatever goods, gear, debts, sums of money, principal, sums, @rents [= annual rents, i.e. interest payments], penalties and expenses, gold, silver, lying money and bank notes, and all other moveable or heritable funds, subjects, debts, goods or effects of whatever denomination, with all bonds, bills, decreets, tickets, accounts, processes and other vouchers or grounds of debt which shall belong to me [at] the time of my decease, or whereto I may or can then have right any manner of way dispensing with the generality aforesaid and admitting these presents to be as valid as if every particular article comprehended or that can be constructed under the general words and description @mentioned [= afore-mentioned] were herein specially insert[ed] and without prejudice of the said generality,'

Amounts owed to William Ruthven

'I do hereby assign and make over to the said **James Dallas** in trust as aforesaid the several sums of money after-specified:

'The sum of £110 sterling of principal contained in a bond granted by **John Hay of Belton** Esquire and **William Forbes**, writer to the signet, to me, dated the 9th day of February 1762 with the penalty therein contained, and all @rents that shall be due thereon at my death and thereafter till payment.

'The sum of £20 5/- sterling of principal contained in a bill dated the 14th day of September 1762 drawn by me upon and accepted by **James Gibson**, surgeon in Edinburgh, payable three months after date and @rents thereof due at my death and thereafter till payment.

'The sum of £10 2/6 sterling contained in a bill drawn by me upon and accepted [by] **Frederick Rudolph Bruce of Bunzean**, residing in the Castle of Edinburgh, dated the 24th day of August 1749 and interest due and to fall due thereon till payment.

'The sum of 10/- sterling contained in a bill drawn by me upon and accepted by Mr. **William Preston**, writer to the signet, residing at Linlithgow, dated the 22nd day of August 1750 and interest due or to fall due thereon till payment.

'The sum of £5 12/- sterling contained in a bill drawn by me upon and accepted by **James Purves**, writer to the signet, dated the 14th day of December 1762, with all interest due and to fall due thereon.

'The sum of £5 sterling contained in a bill drawn by me upon and accepted by **William Horsburgh**, merchant in Edinburgh, residenter in Canongate, dated the 18th day of December 1756, with all interest due or to fall due thereon till payment.

'The sum of £14 7/4 Scots contained in a bill dated the 7th day of February 1755 drawn by me upon and accepted by **James Leslie junior**, writer in Edinburgh, with the @rents due thereon.

'The sum of 6/- sterling contained in a bill dated the 31st October 1758 drawn by me upon and accepted by **Francis Meston**, writer in Edinburgh, with the @rents due thereon.'

The above bills of exchange are for amounts of money lent by William Ruthven (the drawer) to the various other people (upon whom the bill has been drawn and accepted).

'My concern in a process presently depending before the **Lord Alemoor** at the instance of **Alexander Allison** and me against **Messrs. Fairholm and Malcolm**, merchants in Edinburgh, and the representatives of **John Maclaggan**, writer in Edinburgh.

'The sum of £153 14/8 Scots due to me by **Thomas Bruce**,

Deputy Clerk of [the Court of] Session, account for which I have raised a process against him before the Court of Session.

'Whatever balance may happen to be found due to me by **James Gibson**, surgeon in Edinburgh, on selling the accounts betwixt him and me of my intromissions as his factor, in case the balance shall be in my favour.

'Two shares in the Edinburgh Whale Fishing Company and some shares in the Jamaica Company, together with the bond, bills, accounts and processes @mentioned and all diligence and execution respectively following thereon, surrogating and substituting the said **James Dallas** as trustee foresaid in my full right and place of the premises, with full power to him after my death to intromit with uplift and receive and discharge the foresaid debts, sums of money and other moveables generally and particularly above assigned and disponed and, if need be, to pursue therefore decreets to recover and put in execution, as also with power to submit and refer, compone [= pay to a feudal superior], transact, settle and agree there-anent [= concerning] as he shall think proper and every other thing in the premises to do, use and exercise as full and freely as I can do myself in my own life, secluding always my executors and next of kin from the same, and for rendering these presents the more effectual,

'I hereby name and appoint the said **James Dallas** my trustee foresaid, with and under the conditions, provisions and declarations after-specified, my sole executor, universal legatee and intromitter with my haill moveables and executry after my death, and which trust I have vested in the said **James Dallas**, that he may as far as my funds which he shall recover shall extend, after deduction and allowance of the expenses and charges of management and a gratification as after-mentioned, pay my funeral charges in the first place and my just and lawful debts, and in case of a reversion after payment of my said funeral and debts, that he may pay or denude the same as follows:

'the one half of the said reversion to and in favour of the said **Thomas Ruthven**, wigmaker in London, who shall, by receiving thereof, be obliged to pay to **William Ruthven**, shoemaker in London, my natural son, ten pounds sterling;

'and the other half of the said reversion to and in favour of the said **David, Elizabeth** and **Margaret Ruthven** and **Thomas Ruthven**, writer in Edinburgh, equally amongst them.'

'I do not intend that the said **James Dallas** should be put to or incur any loss or inconvenience by executing this my settlement as trustee foresaid. Therefore I hereby declare that his acting in virtue hereof shall not subject him to be liable for any omissions, neglects, errors or mistakes whatever in the execution hereof, but only for his actual intromissions [= taking up and management of the property] after allowance of all payments of debts due by me which he is hereby impowered to settle and adjust as he thinks proper and of all his charges, expenses, fees of writings, agents and layers [lawyers'] fees and a suitable gratification for his own extraordinary trouble.

'The accounts of all which are to be settled and cleared on his own honest word or his oath if required allenarly [= exclusively], reserving also to me full power to revoke, alter or innovate these presents in whole or in part and to use and dispose of my said goods, gear, debts and funds generally and particularly above conveyed in my lifetime as I shall think proper and I dispense with the not delivery here of declaring these presents though found lying by me or in the custody of any personal or after my death to be as valid and effectual to all intents and purposes as if the same were instantly delivered, any law, statute or practice to the contrary notwithstanding.

'And I consent to the registration hereof in the books of Council and Session or others competent therein to remain for preservation and, if need be, that Letters of Horning [= a legal action to compel a defaulting party to pay a debt or carry out an action] on six days charge and all other executionals needful be direct hereon in form as effeirs [= relating to] and thereto I constitute **Robert Gray** my procurator of resignation [= the representative of a feudal vassal charged with restoring the vassal's lands to his superior].

'In witness whereof these presents wrote upon this and the three preceding pages of stamped paper by **John Chalmers**, writer in Edinburgh, are subscribed [= signed] by me at

Edinburgh the 25th day of January 1763 before these witnesses: **James Fogo**, writer in Edinburgh, and the said **John Chalmers**, writer hereof.

'(Signed) W Ruthven, James Fogo, witness, John Chalmers, witness.'

Confirmatory section
This will is unusual in lacking a confirmatory section. Most wills have a section stating that, in the presence of a specified commissioner appointed by the relevant commissary (in this case, the Commissary of Edinburgh), a certain person had appeared before him and had solemnly sworn:

- that (for instance) his father had died on such-and-such a date;
- that he (the son) had entered into possession or management of the deceased's personal or moveable estate as sole executor nominated by his father in his will of such-and-such a date;
- that he (the son) knew of no will other than the one being put forward;
- that the preceding inventory was a full and complete inventory of his father's personal estate and effects, wherever situated;
- that the value of the deceased's personal estate and effects in Scotland was above (for instance) £1,000 sterling and below (for instance) £1,500 sterling;
- and that all of the above was true, as he (the son) should answer to God.

11.2 Inventories
William Ruthven junior, Principal Clerk of the High Court of Admiralty of Scotland from June 1754, was my first cousin seven times removed. He was also the son of the above-mentioned William Ruthven, and died suddenly in March 1757, predeceasing his father.

Transcript of the testament testamentar and inventory of William Ruthven, Reference CC8/8/116, Edinburgh Commissary Court, 1757:

'**In the dining room**
A mahogany clothes chest £3;
A large mahogany dining table £2;
A lesser ditto 18/-;

Eight leather-bottomed mahogany chairs and two elbow ditto (@ 16/- each) £8;
A large chimney glass £3;
A mahogany tea table 12/-;
A large iron chimney fender, poker and tongs £1 5/-;
A new carpet £1;
40 framed prints or pictures £7 7/2.

In the green room
A mahogany bedstead with green moreen [a wool/cotton fabric] curtains and cover £5;
A green moreen curtain for the door, with leads, pulley, etc 6/-;
An easy chair mahogany covered with green damask and with green stuff slip 15/-;
Six elm chairs with green damask bottoms and stuff slip 15/-;
A chimney glass £3;
A wainscot chest of drawers and escritoire 15/-;
A fir repository for books and papers 4/-;
A mahogany clossbox [commode] 10/-;
An iron chimney £1;
A tea chest 5/-;
A mahogany tea board 3d.

In the bedroom
A beech bedstead with Saxon blue moreen mounting £5;
A mahogany half chest of drawers £1 5/-;
A French easy chair of mahogany covered with check 15/-;
A check window curtain with leads, pulley, etc 12/-;
A backgammon table with men, boxes and dice 7/6;
A chimney mounted with brass fender, poker, tongs and shovel 15/-;
A carpet, very small, 5/-.

In the room off the kitchen
A fir press [= cupboard] bed 10/-;
A trunk 4/-;
A press for linen 3/-;
Three fir presses for papers 7/6;
A screen 1/6.

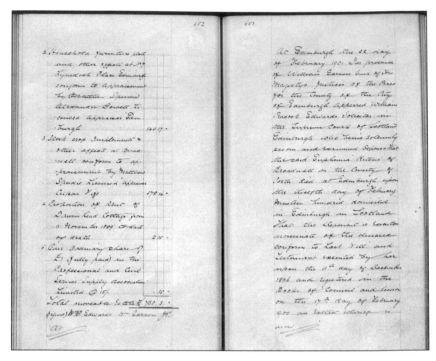

Inventory, 1901. (Crown Copyright, National Records of Scotland, SC70/1/398.)

In the room beyond the kitchen
A fir press bed with green hangings 10/-;
A mahogany cupboard 10/-;
A wainscot table 5/-;
A large chimney with iron sides 9/-;
A cran [frame to support a pot over a fire] 7/-;
A [pair of] tongs 6d;
A fire shovel 1/6;
A coal case 6d;
Two branders 1/2;
A dropping pan and standard 1/6;
An iron spoon 2d;
A heater 4d;
Three smoothing irons and standard 2/2;

A flesh fork 4d;
A frying pan 1/-;
A coffee toaster 1/-;
A bottle brush and corkscrew 1½d;
A chopping knife 6d;
Collop tongs 3d;
A candle box 6d;
A filter 1½d;
A flamer 2d;
A salt box 1½d;
A grater 2d;
A pepper box and flour box 3d;
An oven and pan and pudding pan 2/6;
A drainer 2d;
A toaster 1d;
Eight canisters 1/6;
One large sugar box and little toaster 1/-;
A black decanter 2d;
An oil measure ½d;
A lantern 2/-;
A copper tea kettle 2/-;
A brass ditto and winter 6/-;
A copper coffee pot 4/-;
A copper pot, lid and checks 7/-;
A ditto pan 1/6;
A brass pan 3/-;
A copper goblet, pan and lid 2/6;
A brass pestle and mortar 2/6;
A copper back 10/-;
Six broth plates, 12 plain ditto, one large plate, one broth ditto,
four ashets, choppin flagon, a bathing basin and mustard pot, all
of pewter (@ 18d per pound) weighing [blank];
A painted fir press 3/-;
A jar with lead within and small pan 7/-;
Three kitchen chairs, old and broken, 1/-;
A stool 2d;
A small bottle rack 1/-;
An old knife box 1d;

Sixteen horn-hafted knives and forks 1/-;
A timber basket 2d;
Five tubs 1/-;
Three brushes (a flesh brush and two shoe brushes) 2/-;
A sharpening board for knives 3d;
Two besoms (one hearth besom and one washing) and one hard rubber 2/6;
A butter kit and leet 3d;
A wainscot cheesebox 1/6;
A lemon squeezer 1d;
A hairsearch ½d;
Two lignum vitae candlesticks and one double and two single standards 8/-;
A boot jack 2d.

Follows china
Twelve coloured and gilded china plates, six whereof whole, 12/-;
A blue and white china mug, cracked, 2/6;
Two punch bowls and one clasped 11/-;
Two small bowls, one clasped, 1/-;
Nine cups and two saucers English china 4/-;
Two coloured and gilded mugs, one whereof clasped, and two blue ditto 7/-;
A butter plate and sugar bowl 1/-;
Five delft ashets [large shallow oval dishes, the word deriving from the French assiette] 1/6;
Three stone custard cups 2d.

Follows body clothes
Two priest grey coats 14/-;
Two black cloth vests 5/-;
Five cloth coloured coats, one of them with pebble buttons set in silver, £2 2/-;
Three cloth coloured vests 4/6;
Two black cut velvet vests and one black silken ditto old 7/-;
Three pairs black breeches 6/-;
Seven cloth coloured ditto 14/-;
A grey upper coat 7/-;

A red cloak £1;

Nine pairs coloured stockings and two pairs black ditto (@ 6d per pair) 5/6;

12 under pairs of stockings and a riding pair (@ 3d per pair) 3/3;

22 pairs of thread stockings, seven pairs whereof new, £2 2/-;

One pair of green thread stockings 1/6;

One pair of brown silk stockings 2/6;

One pair of leather gloves and two right hand gloves 4d;

A pair worsted gloves 2d;

42 ruffled shirts (@ 2/6 each) £5 5/- [should be £10 5/-];

Six plain day shirts (@ 2/6 each) 15/-;

Eight nightshirts 8/-;

27 stocks (@ 2d each) 4/6;

25 diaper nightcaps (@ 3d each) 6/3;

Four woollen half caps 4d;

Two old half cotton nightcaps 1d;

16 spotted and one chequered silk napkins, very old, (@ 3d each) 4/- [should be 4/3];

Three cotton pocket napkins and seven linen ditto 3/4;

A pair of black gloves 1d;

Five pairs shoes and two pairs boxes, two pairs boots and one pair straps 15/-;

A cloak bag and six bags for shirts 3/-;

Two pairs weepers 4d;

Wig box and wig 5/-;

A pair red slippers 6d;

An old hat 6d;

A cloth Bavarian coat 10/-.

Follows particulars in Trustees' Office

A press bed and curtains 10/-;

A feather bed 15/-;

A wainscot desk with shuttles 5/-;

A weather glass £1 5/-;

A small fir press 1/-;

17 dozen of choppin [four-pint] bottles (@ 1/- per dozen) 17/-;

Two dozen mutchkin [quarter-pint] bottles (@ 8d per dozen) 1/4.

Follows glasses
Five strong ale glasses (@ 5d per pair) 1/0½;
Three strong ale glasses worm-stalked (@ 2½d) 7½d;
Four plain punch glasses (@ 3d per pair) 6d;
Two other glasses, one cracked, 2d;
12 wine glasses (@ 3d per pair) 1/6;
Two tumbler glasses 4d;
One crystal water bottle 2d;
One lesser water crystal ditto 2d;
Two crystal vinegar cruets 6d.

Follows bed and table linen
One damask table cloth 16/-;
One diaper [cotton/linen cloth with a diamond pattern] ditto and
12 napkins 16/-;
An eternity table cloth 4/-;
11 diaper ditto (@ 3/- each) £1 13/-;
One dozen diaper napkins 6/-;
11 ditto 5/6;
Four lacy napkins 2/6;
13 napkins of different patterns 3/-;
Six towels 3/-;
10 ditto 2/-;
A pair of sheets 10/-;
Two pairs ditto (@ 12/- each) £1 4/-;
Three pairs of sheets (@ 14/- each) £2 2/-;
A pair ditto 7/-;
Two dittoes (10/- each) £1 10/- [should be £1];
Four pairs ditto (@ 9/- each) £1 16/-;
Three pairs ditto (@ 6/- each) 18/-;
Three pairs ditto (@ 6/- each) 18/-;
Five pairs ditto (@ 5/- each) £1 5/-;
One pair ditto, old, 7/-;
Three pairs ditto 4/-;
10 pillow cases (@ 8d each) 6/8;
Eight ditto (@ 5d each) 3/4.

Follows blankets
Three pairs English blankets (@ 8/-) £1 4/-;
Five pairs ditto (@ 6/-) £1 10/-;
Two pairs ditto (@ 6/-) 12/-;
Four pairs ditto (@ 3/-) 12/-;
Three pairs Scots ditto (@ 3/-) 9/-;
Three pairs ditto (@ 2/6 each) 7/6;
Two pairs ditto (@ 3/-) 6/-;
Two pairs ditto (@ 5/-) 10/-;
Two pairs ditto (@ 3/- each) 6/-.

Follows feather beds
A feather bed, bolster and two pillows £1;
Another ditto £1;
A feather mattress, pillow and bolster 10/-;
A small woollen mattress and like for a bolster 5/-;
A feather bed, bolster and two pillows £1 10/-;
A feather bed, bolster and two pillows £2;
A hair mattress 12/-;
A feather bed, bolster and pillow 15/-;
10 spindles of two-up yarn (@ 2/6) £1 5/-;
21 yards of linen (@ 1/6 per yard) £1 11/6;
10¾ yards diaper (@ 10d) 8/11½;
20 yards ditto (@ 1/- per yard) £1.

In the cellar
A bottle rack six foot by two and one half of four storeys 2/6;
23 choppin bottles of whisky and three pints ditto (@ 1/3 [each])
£1 12/6;
34 bottles rum (@ 2/6 per pint) £2 2/6;
Seven dozen choppin bottles of strong ale (@ 2/- per dozen) and
five pint bottles and five mutchkin ditto 16/-.

In the pantry
Five mutchkin bottles of Madera (@ 6d per mutchkin bottle) 2/6;
A cane with china head 1/-;
A whalebone horse whip 1/6.

In the Admiralty Office
15 strong boxes for papers £12;
A press [cupboard] £1;
A clossbox [commode] 7/6;
Two writing desks with leather covers and two stools £2 10/-;
Two copper plates £1;
A grate, poker, tongs and fender 15/-;
A horse whip with silver head 1/-.

All sterling money, extending the values and prices of the goods and gear before-mentioned in haill [in total] to the sum of £139 17/4 sterling, and which were so valued by Katharine Mein, spouse to James Dalgleish, shoemaker, ordinary rouping woman [a woman who bought and sold second-hand furniture] in Edinburgh, conform to her signed estimation thereof of date the fifth day of May 1757 years.

Follows the defunct's silver plate, watch, etc;
A dividing spoon weighing seven ounces twelve drop (@ 5/3 per ounce) £2;
A punch spoon weighing one ounce four drop (@ 5/- per ounce) 6/3;
Six table spoons weighing 15 ounces (@ 5/2 per ounce) £3 7/6;
Five teaspoons weighing one ounce 15 drop (@ 5/- per ounce) 9/8½;
Four bottle bags weighing one and a half ounces (@ 5/4 per ounce) 9/-;
A jug weighing six ounces nine drop (@ 5/2 per ounce) £1 12/11;
Sugar tongs weighing one ounce 15 drop (@ 5/- per ounce) 9/8½;
Two salts and three shovels weighing eight ounces four drop (@ 5/4 per ounce) £2 4/4;
Five breakfast silver-hafted knives seven ounces three drop (@ 5/- per ounce) £1 15/10;
Six silver-hafted knives and forks [weighing] 12 ounces 12 drop (@ 5/- per ounce) £3 3/9;
A gold ring with yellow sielstone [seal-stone, i.e. a signet ring] 12/-;
A medal of Sir Isaac Newton weighing 1¼ ounces (@ 5/4 per ounce) 6/8;
A revolution medal 5/-;
Two silver spurs weighing four ounces four drop (@ 5/- per

ounce) £1 1/3;
Pair of shoe buckles [weighing] 1½ ounces (@ 5/-) 7/6;
A shell snuff box set with silver 6/-;
12 pebble buttons set in silver 6/-;
A horse whip with silver head 1/-;
A fine seal set in gold with a shagreen case £1;
A silver watch £3;

All sterling money, extending the values and prices of the silver plate before-mentioned in haill [in total] to the sum of £23 14/5 sterling, and which silver watch and others before-written were so valued by John Clark, goldsmith in Edinburgh, conform to his signed estimation thereof of date the 13th day of April 1757 years.

Follows the defunct's books
[103 books in 236 volumes are listed individually, including many on the law, business, travel and history.

Also among Ruthven's books is George Mackenzie, 1st Earl of Cromartie's *Account of Gowrie's Conspiracy* (Edinburgh, 1713), about the alleged conspiracy at Gowrie House in Perth in August 1600 against King James VI of Scotland by the 3rd Earl of Gowrie and his brother Alexander Ruthven. William Ruthven's grandfather and great-grandfather were tenants of the Ruthvens of Freeland, a junior branch of the Gowrie line, and may even have been related to them.

William Ruthven Jr also owned the *History of the House of Douglas* (two volumes, Edinburgh, 1743), which was written by David Hume of Godscroft in 1625 and first published about 1633, and is credited as being the first family history printed.]

And which books were valued in whole at the sum of £30 sterling money by Lauchlan Hunter and John Trail, booksellers in Edinburgh, conform to their signed estimation thereof of date the 11th day of April 1757 years.

Item cash lying by the defunct at his death £11 11/2 sterling money, extending the foresaid household, furniture, silver plate, watch, books and lying money before mentioned in whole to the sum of £200 2/11 sterling money, and in Scots money to the sum of £2,461 15/-.'

Chapter 12

INHERITANCE RECORDS, ETC

12.1 Retours/services of heirs

Land and buildings were considered 'heritable', as opposed to 'moveable' property under Scots Law. Moveable property could be bequeathed through a will (a testament testamentar), heritable property could not until the Heritable Jurisdictions Act of 1868.

Land and buildings had to be passed on according to the Scottish law of inheritance. The basic premise of this was that the eldest son succeeded to his father or mother's property. In the absence of a son, the property would be divided equally among any daughters, who were then known as 'heirs portioner'. If there were no children at all, the deceased's next younger brother would succeed as 'heir of line' to inherited property, and the next older brother as 'heir of conquest' to land or buildings that the deceased had purchased.

Before 1847, anyone wishing to inherit land and buildings in Scotland would (although not in all cases) be 'served heir' to the deceased person by means of a *retour* (French for 'return'), which contained the verdict of a jury of people known to the claimant. A 'special' *retour* gives the name of the land, while a 'general' *retour* doesn't.

After 1847, a different system operated, under which a claimant issued a 'petition of service' to either a local court or the Sheriff in Chancery. If the claim were successful, the claimant would be issued a 'decree of service' by either the sheriff of the county or the Sheriff in Chancery.

After 1863, four volumes of ten-year indexes of the services of heirs were published, covering the period 1 January 1700 to 31 December 1859. Unlike the *retours*, the indexes are written in English. They give the date of service and date of recording, which may be many years later.

Here are a few examples from the main indexes:

'Hendry – Isobel, Daughter of Wm. Hendry, Mercht., Edinr., [served heir] to her Grandfather Capt. James Hendry, Mercht. there – Co-heir of Prov. Gl. – [Date of recording] 1755, April 17. [also co-heirs, her brother James and sisters Jean and Marion]'

'Rodger – William, Labourer, Edinburgh, [served heir] to his brother Alexander Rodger, Shoemaker there – Heir of Conquest General – 3 July 1826 – [Date of recording] 1826, July 12.'

'Jacque – Margaret, Wemyss Place, Edinburgh, [served heir] to her Brother Robert Jacque, Demerara – Co-heir General – Dated 23 February 1852. [Date of recording] 1852, Feb. 28.
Jacque – Margaret, above-designed, [served heir] to her Brother James Jacque, Merchant, Gateside – Co-heir General – Dated 23 February 1852. [Date of recording] 1852, Feb. 28.
[also co-heir, her sister Cleland, Widow of David M. Craig, Writer, Largs]'

Although these indexes are alphabetical by the surname of the heir (the person served), supplementary indexes provide the surnames of the person being served to (i.e. the deceased) in all those cases where the surnames are not the same.

Here are some examples from the supplementary indexes:

'1720-1729 [Name of the person served heir to:] M'Kay – Elizabeth – (or *Henderson*) – Widow of Daniel M'Kay, Innkeeper in Edinburgh.
[Name of the heir:] Bell – Elizabeth – (or *Brodie*) – her Niece.'

'1790-1799 [Name of the person served heir to:] Ruthven – Thomas – Writer in Edinburgh.
[Name of the heir:] Bayne – Ann and Margaret, his Nieces.'

'1810-1819 [Name of the person served heir to:] Crawford – John – Shipmaster in Leith.
[Name of the heir:] Fachney – James – his Grandnephew.'

(In the second example above, Ann Bayne was my four times great-grandmother. This entry subsequently led me to the will of Thomas Ruthven, which contained a lot of information that was very useful to me.)

The *retours*/services of heirs are held by the National Records of Scotland, but have not been put online. All four volumes of the ten-year indexes from 1700-1859 have been digitised, however, and made available on a CD published by the Scottish Genealogy Society (see Appendix 6). In addition, the society has issued a CD of printed summaries of earlier *retours*, covering the period 1545-1699. The summaries are in Latin, apart from those from the years 1652-1659 when Scotland was part of Oliver Cromwell's Commonwealth of England, Scotland and Ireland.

Here is an example of a summary in English (with original spellings):

'Dec. 9 1658
BEATRIX SALMOND spous to James Tailyifer [Telfer] merchand burges of Edinburgh, and JANET SALMOND spous to John Robertsone merchand ther, *heirs portioners* of William Salmond son to Robert Salmond merchand burges of Edinburgh, *their brother* – in tenements in Edinburgh. E. 3s. 4d.'

And one in Latin:

'Maii 28 1646
ANDREAS FRASER mercator Cracoviensis, *haeres* Gilberti Fraser mercatoris burgensis de Edinburgh, *fratris germani* – in tenementis in Edinburgh. E. 3s. 4d. – Annuo redditu 40s. de tenemento in Edinburgh – Annuo redditu 13s. 4d. de tenemento in Edinburgh.'

'[Translation:
May 28 1646
ANDREW FRASER merchant in Cracow, *heir* of Gilbert Fraser merchant burgess of Edinburgh, *his brother* – in tenements in Edinburgh. E. 3s. 4d. [The 'E' is an abbreviation for 'extent', meaning value.] – Annual rent 40s. for a tenement in Edinburgh – Annual rent 13s. 4d. for a tenement in Edinburgh.]

12.2 Sasines – land transfers

Until 2004, land and buildings were held in Scotland under the feudal system, whereby they were not owned outright but held in a pyramid-like structure under the Crown. The people at the bottom of the pyramid were known as 'vassals' and those directly above them were their 'feudal superiors', to whom the vassals had to pay 'feu duty' (a tax in lieu of the military service they would at one time have been obliged to provide).

This arrangement came to an end on 28 November 2004, when the Abolition of Feudal Tenure (Scotland) Act 2000 came into operation. Now land and buildings in Scotland are owned outright by the former vassals, while feudal superiors and feu duty have been abolished.

Under the old system, the heir to a vassal could prove his right to inherit land and buildings by obtaining a *retour* or 'service of heir' (see above). Whether the property had been inherited or purchased, the transfer of ownership of the land needed to be recorded in the appropriate 'sasine' (pronounced '*say-zin*') register.

The National Records of Scotland (NRS) points out in its online guide to sasines (at www.nrscotland.gov.uk/research/guides/sasines) that before the twentieth century, most people in Scotland were tenants rather than owners of buildings or farm-land. Therefore you will not find those people (the majority of our ancestors) in either the registers of sasines or the records of services of heirs.

In 1599, an attempt was made to register sasines in what became known as the 'Secretary's Register' (SR), which was abandoned ten years later. In 1617, sasine registration began again with 'particular registers' (PRs) of sasines kept for most counties (those for Edinburgh City and Midlothian cover the periods 1617-1700 and 1741-1780) and also a 'general register of sasines' covering all of Scotland except West, Mid and East Lothian. The particular and general registers were replaced in 1869 by one general register in county divisions. In addition, the sixty-six 'royal burghs' of Scotland (which included Edinburgh and Queensferry) kept their own sasine registers.

The NRS states that the sasine registers are 'fairly complete' from 1617 and 'fully comprehensive' from about 1660. Where an eldest son inherited a property, however, he might have simply continued to live in the family home and not have bothered to have a sasine executed until a far later date.

Beginning with Renfrewshire on 6 April 1981, the registers of sasines were replaced by a Scottish national Land Register, with the final six historic counties becoming operational on the new register on 1 April 2003. West Lothian moved to the Land Register on 1 October 1993 and Midlothian on 1 April 2001.

All the sasines in the general and particular registers (but not the burgh registers) have been digitised and are available to view on 'virtual volumes' at the NRS, which provides an electronic index to the sasines from 1781 onwards. Summaries of the sasines, known as 'abridgements', are also in the electronic index.

12.3 Landed estate records
Although the core area of Edinburgh has been urban for centuries, most of the present City of Edinburgh unitary authority area consisted of rural parishes in the counties of Midlothian and West Lothian. There may well be papers relating to landed estates owned by your ancestors, or more probably estates on which they worked or were tenants, as is the case in my family tree.

You may find these records in the online catalogues of the National Records of Scotland (http://tinyurl.com/NRSonlinecat), the Scottish Archive Network (www.scan.org.uk/catalogue) for Edinburgh City Archives and the other archives listed at the end of Chapter 8, and the National Register of Archives for Scotland, (http://tinyurl.com/NRAScotland).

12.4 Fatal accident inquiries
Unlike England, Wales and Northern Ireland, Scotland has no coroners' courts. Instead, a procurator fiscal (a public prosecutor) investigates accidental, unexpected, unexplained, sudden or suspicious deaths.

In Scotland, deaths have to be registered within eight days, but the cause of death may not have been determined by that time. An investigation, known as a precognition, is carried out for the procurator fiscal and its findings are noted briefly in the Register of Corrected Entries (RCE) (see Chapter 7). The National Records of Scotland (NRS) holds procurator fiscal records for Edinburgh from 1870-1896 (NRS reference AD19, where 'AD' stands for Lord Advocate's Department).

If an RCE note refers to a 'jury', then a Fatal Accident Inquiry (FAI, held since 1895) is likely to have taken place in a sheriff court with a jury. The scope of an FAI was widened in 1906 to include inquiries into sudden or suspicious deaths. From 1976 onwards, a jury was no longer required and the FAI system was extended to cover deaths in prisons, within legal custody and in the offshore oil industry.

FAIs are relatively rare and, while they do investigate industrial accidents, they don't cover suicides or road traffic deaths. You can search all the FAI records held by the NRS (many have not survived) by the names of the deceased in its online catalogue, http://tinyurl.. com/NRSonlinecat.

You may find earlier fatal accidents (before the introduction of the inquiry system in 1895) in the Lord Advocate's Department records, including the registers of sudden deaths, fatal accident inquiries and accidents in mines 1848-1935 (NRS reference AD12). Don't forget to look in local and national newspapers, where you may well find much more information than has survived in the official records.

The (mostly unindexed) Annual Returns and Reports on Railway Accidents published by the Ministry of Transport for the years 1854-1856, 1861-1940 and 1947 are held by the NRS (reference BR/MT/ S/6/1-132) and listed in its catalogue.

The NRS also holds indexed Official Accident Reports for incidents that took place on the North British Railway from 1869-1897 (BR/MT/S/6/135-6) and individual accidents on British Railways (Scottish Region) from 1951-1975 (BR/MT/S/6137-166). In addition, some of the railway companies maintained their own books of accidents, which you can find in the NRS catalogue by searching the reference 'BR' for 'accident book'.

Chapter 13

EDINBURGH'S CIVIL AND CRIMINAL COURTS

When Scotland was united with England in 1707, the Treaty of Union stipulated that Scotland would retain its own laws and legal system, and it still does to this day. Scotland kept its own system of courts, which differed from the English and Welsh system, and instead of having barristers and solicitors Scotland retained its advocates and writers. The latter are nowadays known as solicitors, although many of them are members of the Society of Writers to the Signet, who use the initials 'W.S.' on their door-plates. The society dates back to 1594, although the earliest recorded use of the Signet (the private seal of the early Scottish kings) was in 1369.

The National Records of Scotland (NRS) holds records of the Scottish law courts, including those of the courts described below: the Court of Session; the High Court of Justiciary; Admiralty Court; Exchequer Court; the sheriff courts; the commissary courts; and the Justice of the Peace courts.

The NRS has made available online various guides to the records of the Scottish civil and criminal courts, including:

- Court of Session Records, www.nrscotland.gov.uk/research/guides/court-of-session-records;
- High Court Criminal Trials, www.nrscotland.gov.uk/research/guides/high-court-criminal-trials;
- Commissary Court Records, www.nrscotland.gov.uk/research/guides/commissary-court-records;
- Sheriff Court Records, www.nrscotland.gov.uk/research/guides/sheriff-court-records;
- Justices of the Peace Records, www.nrscotland.gov.uk/research/guides/justices-of-the-peace-records.

13.1 The Court of Session

The Court of Session and the High Court of Justiciary are the highest level courts in Scotland. They are housed within the old Parliament House in Edinburgh, built between 1631 and 1640 for the old Scottish Parliament and where it sat prior to the union with England.

Established in 1532, the Court of Session is Scotland's highest civil court, of which the most senior judges are the Lord President and the Lord Justice-Clerk. Its decisions can be the subject of an appeal to the Supreme Court in London, since the latter was set up in October 2009. Prior to that date, an appeal could be made to the House of Lords in London. Over time, the court has absorbed the functions of the Scottish Court of Admiralty (in 1830), some of the functions of the commissary courts (in 1836, although their testamentary functions had passed to the sheriff courts), and the Scottish Court of Exchequer (in 1856).

13.2 The High Court of Justiciary

Set up in 1672 to replace earlier Justiciars' courts, the High Court of Justiciary is Scotland's highest-level criminal court, from which there is no appeal to the Supreme Court in London. The same judges who sit in the Court of Session for civil matters also sit in the High Court to hear criminal cases. The Lord President of the Court of Session is also Lord Justice General when sitting in the High Court.

The court deals with significant cases such as murder, sitting in Edinburgh, Glasgow and Aberdeen, as well as going 'on circuit' throughout Scotland as necessary.

13.3 The Sheriff Courts

The sheriff courts deal with both criminal and civil cases, including the confirmation of testaments after 1836 (1823 outside the Lothians). The office of sheriff ('shire reeve') was introduced to Scotland by King David I in the twelfth century, as an official responsible for keeping the king's peace in a shire (or county). At that time, a sheriffdom and shire were synonymous.

Up to 1747, the office of sheriff was hereditary in twenty-two of the sheriffdoms, three sheriffs were appointed for life, and eight (including the Sheriff of Edinburgh) were appointed by the monarch. The sheriff would often appoint a sheriff depute to hear cases, and a sheriff substitute to take the sheriff depute's place when he was unavailable.

After the Jacobite Rebellion of 1745-1746, hereditary sheriffs were abolished and sheriffs depute became known simply as sheriffs. In 1971, sheriffs and sheriffs substitute were renamed sheriffs principal and sheriff respectively.

In 1872, Midlothian and Haddington (East Lothian) were combined to form one sheriffdom, to which Linlithgow (West Lothian) was added in 1881 and Peebles in 1883. Since 1975, Scotland has been divided into only six sheriffdoms, one of which is Lothian and the Borders (covering the City of Edinburgh, Midlothian, East Lothian, West Lothian and Scottish Borders unitary authorities).

Today, Edinburgh Sheriff Court sits in a large building in Chambers Street, which opened to the public in 1994.

13.4 The Commissary Courts

The commissary courts were set up between 1564 and 1566, when Scotland changed State religion from Roman Catholicism to Protestantism. The areas under their jurisdiction were called 'commissariots' and they were based on the pre-Reformation Catholic dioceses.

The jurisdiction of the principal court, the Commissary Court of Edinburgh, covered the Lothians (and originally also covered Peeblesshire and part of Stirlingshire). This court dealt with cases relating to marriage, divorce, separation and legitimacy, as well as confirmation of testaments, including those of people who had died outside Scotland ('furth of Scotland') and had moveable estate there. The other twenty-one commissary courts dealt mainly with the confirmation of testaments and registration of inventories. These courts were abolished as separate courts in 1823 and their testamentary functions passed to the sheriff courts.

The Commissary Court of Edinburgh lost its non-testamentary functions to the Court of Session in 1830, and its testamentary function to the sheriff courts in 1836.

13.5 The Admiralty and Exchequer Courts

As well as the courts mentioned above, there was also the High Court of Admiralty, which sat in Edinburgh and dealt with criminal and civil maritime cases. These included crime on the high seas, and disputes between merchants and mariners. The court was abolished in 1830 and its civil jurisdiction was transferred to the Court of Session.

The Court of Exchequer was set up after the Union of the Parliaments in 1707, and dealt with revenue cases, such as those involving smuggling and illicit production of beer and spirits. In 1856, the court's jurisdiction passed to the Court of Session.

13.6 Local courts
There were also several local Edinburgh courts dealing with civil matters and minor criminal offences, such as the Justice of the Peace (JP) Court, dealing with riots and minor criminal offences, as well as regulating highways, bridges and ferries, and the Burgh (or Bailie) Court of Edinburgh, which dealt with civil matters. There was also the Ten Mark Court, dealing with small claims, and the Dean of Guild Court for building matters.

The Leith, Canongate and Portsburgh Burgh (or Bailie) Courts all had jurisdiction over both criminal and civil matters. Queensferry also had a Burgh Court. From 1805, Edinburgh also had a Police Court.

These local courts were replaced by a District Court in 1975, but the Justice of the Peace Court was re-instated in 2008 in the same building as Edinburgh Sheriff Court.

The National Records of Scotland (NRS) holds records of the:

- Edinburgh Justice of the Peace Courts, 1613-1967;
- Midlothian Justice of the Peace Courts, 1708-1975.

Edinburgh City Archives hold the records of the following local courts:

- Edinburgh Burgh Court, 1507-1828;
- Canongate Burgh Court, 1569-1863;
- Leith Burgh Court, 1624-1920;
- Queensferry Burgh Court, 1661-1966.

13.7 Prisons and prisoners
The Old Tolbooth
The first known documentary reference to the Old Tolbooth dates from 1368, and it was once Edinburgh's main municipal building. Situated next to St Giles' Cathedral, as well as being the city's main gaol the Tolbooth was home to the Burgh Council, the Scottish Parliament and the Court of Session.

Although the council, parliament and court had already moved out to newer buildings, the Old Tolbooth continued to be used as a prison until it was demolished in 1817. The position of its doorway is marked in the High Street by a heart shape, formed by coloured setts (granite blocks) in the roadway. The Tolbooth's actual door and doorway are built into a side wall of Abbotsford, Sir Walter Scott's house, which is situated in the Scottish Borders between Galashiels and Melrose.

Calton Gaol

The Calton Gaol complex consisted of three groups of buildings:

- Calton Bridewell (named after the prison in London), built between 1791 and 1796 on what is now Regent Road, with various workshops;
- Calton Gaol, constructed between 1815 and 1817 to the west of the Bridewell;
- a Debtor's Gaol to the east of the Bridewell, built between 1845 and 1847.

Calton Gaol had the reputation of being a cold and miserable place and it was closed down in 1925, then, apart from the Governor's House, demolished in 1930. The gaol was replaced by St Andrew's House, a Government building, construction for which began in 1936 and was completed by 1939. The graves of ten murderers lie under the St Andrew's House car park. Most of the gaol's rubble was used in the construction of Hopes Reservoir Dam in the Lammermuir Hills, but the door to the death cell is now in the Beehive Inn situated in the Grassmarket.

Saughton Prison

The construction of Edinburgh's present-day gaol, generally known as Saughton Prison, began in 1914 but the prison has been extensively redeveloped in recent years. Saughton received its first prisoner about 1920 and now holds just under 1,000 prisoners, although its official capacity is 872.

Prison records

The NRS holds the following prison records:

- Edinburgh (Calton), 1841-1874;

- Edinburgh (Calton) Bridewell, 1798-1840;
- Edinburgh (Calton) Gaol, 1817-1821;
- Edinburgh (Calton) Prison, 1856-1870;
- Edinburgh (Saughton), 1922-1996;
- Edinburgh Court Buildings Prison, 1858-1862;
- Edinburgh Lock-up House, 1826-1850;
- Edinburgh Police, 1841-1842;
- Edinburgh Tolbooth, 1816-1817;
- Leith Police, 1840-1848.

The NRS also has warding and liberation books from the Old Tolbooth from 1657-1816. Selected entries from these books have been edited by John A Fairley and published in the *Book of the Old Edinburgh Club* (volumes four-six, eight, nine, eleven and twelve). These volumes have been digitised and are available in the Internet Archive, https:// archive.org.

The NRS also holds administrative records for Scottish prisons, which occasionally contain references to individual prisoners. There is also information in the NRS Catalogue on several prisoners, including the following men who were tried and convicted at the High Court in Edinburgh:

- John Watson Laurie, tried in 1889 (HH15/1);
- Hugh Mooney, tried in 1902 (HH15/13);
- Oscar Slater, tried in 1909 (HH15/20/1-3);
- William Drummond Dick, tried in 1914 (HH15/8);
- James Tinsley, tried in 1915 (HH15/10);
- Michael Callaghan, tried in 1918 (HH15/18);
- William Lamb, tried in 1919 (HH15/26).

Chapter 14

TAXING EDINBURGH

The National Records of Scotland (NRS) holds many seventeenth, eighteenth and nineteenth century records of the various forms of taxation described below. The Hearth and Poll Taxes were levied and the Land Tax began to be collected in the seventeenth century, at a time when Scotland had its own parliament.

After the Union of the Parliaments of Scotland and England in 1707, the Window Tax was collected from the mid to late eighteenth century, while the other taxes described below date from the late eighteenth century.

You can browse schedules of most of the taxes mentioned below at the subscription-based ScotlandsPlaces website, www.scotlandsplaces .gov.uk.

14.1 Land Tax, 1649-1814

Online at ScotlandsPlaces are 129 volumes of Land Tax rolls for Scotland compiled by the Commissioners of Supply. These rolls, otherwise known as 'cess' or valuation rolls, give the owners (but not the tenants) of landed estates and the rental value of their lands.

The Land Tax rolls for Midlothian cover some of the parishes now within the City of Edinburgh unitary authority for the years 1649, 1680, 1708, 1712, 1726, 1771, 1802 and 1814. The parishes of West Lothian (and now in Edinburgh) are covered for the years 1667 and 1771. The burghs of Edinburgh and Queensferry are not included.

14.2 Hearth Tax, 1691-1695

The NRS holds forty-three volumes of Hearth Tax schedules for Scotland, which are now online at ScotlandsPlaces. In 1690, the Scottish Parliament levied a tax for every hearth (the floor of a fireplace) in Scotland, with only hospitals and the poor exempt. The Scottish Hearth Tax, which was intended to raise money for the army, was imposed later than that of England and Wales, which was collected from 1662-1689.

People were no keener on paying taxes in the past than they are today, and the Government had great difficulty in collecting the Hearth Tax from 1691-1695, particularly in remote areas.

For those counties that listed all taxpayers (as did Mid and West Lothian), the tax schedules function as a heads-of-household census, as the Hearth Tax was payable by both landowners and tenants. Not all schedules were handed in to the Exchequer, and the NRS has Hearth Tax lists that include Edinburgh among its Leven and Melville papers collection.

14.3 Poll Tax, 1693-1699

The Poll Tax was levied on all adults in Scotland, both men and women, who were not in receipt of charity and, like the Hearth Tax, it was difficult to collect.

The NRS holds Poll Tax records for the following parishes now within the City of Edinburgh unitary authority:

- Canongate – naming wives and giving occupations;
- Colinton – naming wives and giving occupations (imperfect);
- Cramond – naming wives and children, and the location of houses;
- Currie – naming wives and giving occupations (imperfect);
- Dalmeny – naming children, and giving occupations and the location of houses;
- Duddingston – giving the locations of houses;
- Edinburgh, College Kirk – naming wives;
- Edinburgh, Greyfriars – naming wives (imperfect);
- Edinburgh, Lady Yester's – naming wives (imperfect);
- Edinburgh, New Kirk – naming children (imperfect);
- Edinburgh, Old Kirk – naming children;
- Edinburgh, Tolbooth – naming wives and children, and giving occupations;
- Edinburgh, Tron – naming wives and children, and giving occupations;
- Kirkliston – naming wives and children, and giving occupations and the locations of houses;
- Leith, North – giving occupations;
- Leith, South – (imperfect);

- Liberton – naming children, and giving occupations and the locations of houses;
- Ratho – naming wives and children, and giving occupations and the locations of houses;
- West Kirk (or St Cuthbert's) – giving occupations and the locations of houses.

14.4 Other taxes, 1747-1802
After Scotland was united with England and Wales as 'Great Britain' in 1707, a number of other taxes were levied on the population of Scotland:

- Window Tax, 1747-1798 – payable by householders on houses with seven or more windows (218 volumes online);

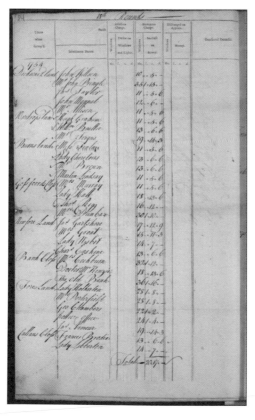

Window tax record, 1754.
(Crown Copyright,
National Records of
Scotland, E326/1/154,
page 24)

Female servant tax record, 1790. (Crown Copyright, National Records of Scotland, E326/6/23, page 82)

- Male Servant Tax, 1777-1798 – payable by employers of male servants, it names the employer and the servant, along with his position (twenty-seven volumes online);
- Inhabited House Tax, 1778-1798 – payable by householders on houses with an annual rental of £5 or more (sixty-four volumes online);

- Commutation Tax, 1784-1798 – payable by householders, it replaced excise duties on tea (not available online);
- Female Servant Tax, 1785-1792 – payable by employers of female servants, it names the employer and the servant (twenty-eight volumes online);
- Shop Tax, 1785-1789 – payable on shops with an annual rental of £5 or more (eight volumes online);
- Cart Tax, 1785-1798 – payable by owners of two-, three- or four-wheeled carts (fourteen volumes online);
- Carriage Tax, 1785-1798 – payable by owners of two- or four-wheeled carriages (twenty volumes online);
- Horse Tax, 1785-1798 – payable by owners of carriage and saddle horses (thirty-three volumes online);
- Farm Horse Tax, 1797-1798 – payable by owners of work horses and mules (thirteen volumes online);
- Dog Tax, 1797-1798 – payable by owners of non-working dogs (two volumes online);
- Consolidated Schedules of Assessed Taxes 1798-1799 – payable by those who paid the above taxes in 1798 (thirty-two volumes online);
- Income Tax, 1799-1802 – payable by those with annual incomes of £60 or more, arising from property or profession, trade or office (not available online).

Chapter 15

EDINBURGH'S SCHOOLS

15.1 The Royal High School

Originally admitting boys only, the Royal High School traces its origins back to a school founded by the canons of Holyrood Abbey in 1128. By 1519, it was known as the Grammar School and situated within a house in Blackfriars Wynd, which had been a palace belonging to Archbishop Beaton at a time when Scotland was still Roman Catholic.

In 1555 the school moved to a house near the head of what was later called High School Wynd. Twenty-three years later, the High School had transferred to a new building in the Blackfriars' cemetery. The area

Royal High School, late nineteenth century. From Edinburgh and its Environs *(Valentine & Sons, c.1901).*

surrounding the school became known as the High School Yards, and almost 200 years later the school moved to another new building nearby.

Between 1825 and 1829, a much grander building was erected in Regent Road, on the south side of the Calton Hill. The new High School was designed by the architect Thomas Hamilton, a former pupil, who is buried in the Old Calton Burial Ground, not far from the school (see Chapter 10). The High School gained the prefix 'Royal' after the future King Edward VII studied under its Rector in 1859.

In 1968, the Royal High moved from the city centre to a suburban location in Barnton, and since 1973 has admitted girls and become a comprehensive school.

15.2 Leith Academy

The earliest mention of the 'grammer scule of Leith' dates back to 1521, and the school was placed in the control of South Leith kirk session in 1560, under which it remained until 1806.

The school was meeting in Trinity House by 1636, where it remained up to 1710. It was then moved to the King James Hospital, located until 1806 within the present South Leith Churchyard. As a result of complaints about damp and unhealthy conditions, the kirk session had a new building constructed on Leith Links, which was used until 1931. In 1888, the school's name was changed to Leith Academy from Leith High School, which it had been known as since 1846.

To relieve overcrowding, a new building was erected in 1931 in Duke Street facing the bottom of Easter Road, and the Leith Links building became Leith Academy Primary (nowadays known simply as Leith Primary). In May 1991, the present Leith Academy was opened between Easter Road and Lochend Road, and the Duke Street building became part of Queen Margaret College (now called Queen Margaret University – see Chapter 16).

15.3 George Heriot's School

George Heriot was goldsmith and banker to King James VI and his Queen Consort, Anne of Denmark. Known as 'Jinglin' Geordie', Heriot died in 1624, leaving over £23,625 to found a 'hospital' for the education of the sons of poor burgesses of Edinburgh.

The construction of the school began in 1629 just outside the city

George Heriot's School, late nineteenth century. From Edinburgh and its Environs *(Valentine & Sons, c.1901).*

walls, next to Greyfriars' Church. The impressive building was used as a military hospital after the Battle of Dunbar in 1650, and the first pupils entered the school in 1659. In 1886, Heriot's became a day school, for boys from seven (since lowered to five, and now four) to university entrance age, and became co-educational in 1979.

15.4 The Mary Erskine School

This fee-paying school for girls is one of four schools run by the Merchant Company of Edinburgh, which was set up in 1681 to protect Edinburgh merchants' trading rights. The school was founded in 1694 in the Cowgate by the Merchant Company, funded by a donation from the widowed Mary Erskine, as the Merchant Maiden 'Hospital' for the education of daughters of burgesses. Mary Erskine was born in Clackmannanshire and, though she was married twice, had no surviving children to inherit the money she made by opening a private bank.

Renamed the Educational Institution for Young Ladies in 1870, the school moved to Queen Street in 1871, after which it was popularly known as Queen Street School. It became Edinburgh Ladies' College in 1889, and in 1944, the Mary Erskine School. In 1966, the school moved to a suburban location at Ravelston and was twinned with Stewart's Melville College (see below) in 1977. The schools share a co-educational primary preparatory school and both have co-educational sixth forms.

15.5 George Watson's College
This co-educational fee-paying school was founded as a charitable 'hospital' for boys in 1738 by the Merchant Company, funded by a bequest from George Watson, an Edinburgh merchant and financier (although not a member of the company).

Watson's opened in 1741 in Lauriston Place, opposite George Heriot's School, and became a day school in 1870. At the same time, the school moved a short distance into the building of the Merchant Maiden Hospital (now the Mary Erskine School – see above), which had moved to Queen Street. In 1927, the Merchant Company bought the site of Merchiston Castle School in Colinton Road, next to Watson's playing fields at Myreside. A new school building, designed by former pupil James B Dunn, was constructed and opened in 1932.

George Watson's College became co-educational when it was combined with its sister school George Watson's Ladies' College in 1974, within an enlarged campus at Colinton Road. The Ladies' College had been founded in 1871 by the Merchant Company, in Melville House, George Square. Originally called George Watson's College School for Young Ladies, it was renamed George Watson's College for Ladies in 1877 and George Watson's Ladies' College in 1890.

15.6 James Gillespie's High School
James Gillespie was an Edinburgh tobacco merchant, whose legacy enabled the Merchant Company to found a school in Bruntsfield Place in 1803, moving to Gillespie Crescent in 1870.

The school had originally been for boys, but girls were also admitted over the years. At that time, Gillespie's acted as a preparatory primary school for the Merchant Company's secondary schools. In 1908, the company handed over responsibility for the school to the Edinburgh School Board, and by 1914, when the school moved into what had been the original Boroughmuir School, it had a secondary department too.

In 1930, the school became James Gillespie's High School for Girls. Five years later, Edinburgh Corporation bought from the Warrender family Bruntsfield House and its grounds, in which a new school was built from 1964 to 1966, with Bruntsfield House as the centrepiece.

From 1973 to 1978, the school became co-educational. A major refurbishment and rebuild programme began in 1987 and was completed in 1991.

15.7 Donaldson's School

In 1850, the school was founded, as Donaldson's Hospital, by Sir James Donaldson, intended as a hospital for destitute and vulnerable children. The palatial original school building in West Coates was designed by the noted Edinburgh architect William Playfair. The governors agreed in 1856 that deaf children should not be excluded, and Donaldson's became primarily a school for deaf children.

The Edinburgh Royal Institution for the Deaf and Dumb was founded in 1810 in Chessel's Court, and later moved to Henderson Row. In 1938, it was merged with Donaldson's, moving during 2008 to a new purpose-built campus in Linlithgow.

15.8 The Edinburgh Academy

This fee-paying school opened in 1824 in Henderson Row to promote classical learning, in particular Greek, which was not taught at the Royal High School (see above) at that time. The school is still in its original home, although several other buildings have been added around it. Originally for boys only, the Edinburgh Academy became a co-educational school in 2008.

15.9 John Watson's Institution

In 1762, John Watson, an Edinburgh Writer to the Signet (solicitor), died leaving a legacy that was eventually used to found what became known as John Watson's Institution in 1828. The school was closed in 1975, however, and its building became the Scottish National Gallery of Modern Art in 1980 (see Appendix 5).

15.10 Stewart's Melville College

This fee-paying boys' school was founded as Daniel Stewart's 'Hospital' by the Merchant Company in 1855, using a fund left by

Daniel Stewart, who had made his money as a merchant in India.

Melville College had originally been founded by the Reverend Robert Cunningham in 1832, as the Edinburgh Institution for Languages and Mathematics'. Its name was changed to Melville College in 1936, owing to the school's location in Melville Street. Daniel Stewart's and Melville College were combined in 1972, then twinned with the Mary Erskine School in 1977 (see above).

15.11 Merchiston Castle School

Five years after Charles Chalmers founded his boys' boarding school in 1828, he leased Merchiston Castle, the former home of John Napier, the inventor of logarithms. At that time, the castle stood in the countryside surrounding Edinburgh. By 1930, the school had outgrown the castle (now the centrepiece of Edinburgh Napier University) and moved to the eighteenth century Colinton House, 3 miles away, which now houses the science department. The school's main block and boarding houses were built in 1930.

15.12 Fettes College

Sir William Fettes, who died in 1836, bequeathed £166,000 to be used to educate poor children and orphans in memory of his only son William, who had died in 1815. Sir William's bequest was invested and later used to buy the land for the school, which opened in 1870.

Originally for boys only, Fettes College has been fully co-educational since 1983. Known as the 'Eton of the North', more than two-thirds of the school's pupils are boarders. Fettes adheres to the English education system of A-Levels and GCSEs, and the International Baccalaureate, rather than the Scottish education system of Advanced Highers, Highers and Nationals.

15.13 Loretto School

Situated just outside Edinburgh, Loretto School is located in Musselburgh, formerly in the county of Midlothian, but in East Lothian since the Scottish local government re-organisation in 1975. Loretto was founded in the 1820s by the Reverend Thomas Langhorne as a day and boarding school for boys. Since 1995, Loretto has been fully co-educational.

Fettes College, late nineteenth century. From Edinburgh and its Environs *(Valentine & Sons, c.1901).*

15.14 Other Edinburgh secondary schools

Other than the Royal High School, Leith Academy and James Gillespie's High School, the schools mentioned above are independent, fee-paying establishments. Other state schools founded in the late nineteenth and early twentieth centuries include: Portobello (founded in 1876); Trinity Academy (1893 as Craighall Road School); Boroughmuir (1904); Broughton (1909); as well as the Roman Catholic schools St Thomas of Aquin's (1886) and Holy Cross Academy (1907, now St Augustine's RC High School).

15.15 Where are the school records located?

Registers and Rolls of Honour
- The register of the Edinburgh Academy (1824-1914) has been published, digitised and made available online at the Internet Archive, https://archive.org.
- In addition, the Internet Archive has Rolls of Honour for George Heriot's School (1914-1919, with many photographs), Loretto School (1914-1920), Merchiston Castle School (1914-1919) and the Royal High School (1914-1918, with many photographs).

- At TheGenealogist, www.thegenealogist.co.uk, you can search and view the registers of Fettes College (1870-1922) and Loretto School (1825-1925), as well as the Royal High School Roll of Honour (1914-1918).
- In the 'Britain, School and University Register Books, 1264-1930' collection at Findmypast.co.uk, www.findmypast.co.uk, you can search and view the registers of the Edinburgh Academy 1824-1914), Loretto School (1825-1925) and Merchiston Castle School (1833-1903).
- Family Relatives, www.familyrelatives.com, has searchable copies of the registers of the Edinburgh Academy (1824-1914) and Loretto School (1825-1948).
- S&N Genealogy Supplies, www.genealogysupplies.com, has published the Edinburgh Academy register (1824-1914) on CD.
- Anguline Research Archives, http://anguline.co.uk/schl.html, has published the registers of Edinburgh Academy (1824-1914), Fettes College (1870-1932), Loretto School (1825-1925) and Merchiston Castle School (1833-1903) in CD and digital download format.
- The National Records of Scotland holds records of George Heriot's School, including admission registers from 1659-1939.
- For records of state schools, you should contact Edinburgh City Archives archives@edinburgh.gov.uk.
- For the records of independent schools that have not published their registers, you should contact the school directly.

School magazine
- You can view many PDF copies of the Leith Academy magazine at the school's website www.leith.edin.sch.uk/magarchive.aspx. The years covered include 1921 and most years from 1948-1980. You'll also find a copy of the special magazine published in 1960 to celebrate 400 years of the school.
- The Internet Archive has digitised copies of the Trinity Academy magazine for 1965 and 1969.

Chapter 16

EDINBURGH'S UNIVERSITIES

16.1 The University of Edinburgh

Founded in 1583, Edinburgh is the fourth oldest of Scotland's ancient universities – the others being St Andrews (founded in 1413), Glasgow (1451), King's College, Aberdeen (1495) and Marischal College, Aberdeen (1593).

Edinburgh University was originally a College of Law, founded as a result of a legacy from Bishop Robert Reid of St Magnus Cathedral in Orkney. It became a university by means of a Royal Charter from King James VI. Until the nineteenth century, the university had no purpose-built campus and used various buildings in the city centre. In 1789, funds were raised to construct a new college (now known as the Old College) to replace the other buildings and work began in that year to a design by the architect Robert Adam.

Adam's death in 1792 and the imposition of Income Tax to pay for the Napoleonic Wars slowed and then halted construction. More funds were raised in 1815 and two years later, William Playfair was appointed as architect, with the college completed in 1827, minus the dome in Adam's design, which was added in 1887.

As the Old College had become overcrowded by the end of the nineteenth century, new Medical School premises were built in the 1870s and the McEwan Hall (a graduating hall) in 1880s. What is now called New College was founded in 1843 as a college of the Free Church of Scotland (see Chapter 9) and merged with the university's Faculty of Divinity (now School of Divinity) in 1935.

The university has continued to expand and now consists of six main campuses:

• The central area – including buildings in George Square and Teviot Place, Old College, New College and the McEwan Hall – which is mainly occupied by the College of Humanities and Social Science;

University of Edinburgh, Old College, late nineteenth century. From Edinburgh and its Environs *(Valentine & Sons, c.1901).*

- King's Buildings, near Blackford Hill, which hold most of the Science and Engineering College;
- The Chancellor's Building in the Royal Infirmary at Little France in Edinburgh's southern suburbs, which houses the Medical School;
- Easter Bush veterinary campus, which is 7 miles south of central Edinburgh, between Loanhead and Milton Bridge;
- Moray House School of Education (formerly Moray House Institute for Education, which merged with the university in 1998).

In 2011, the Edinburgh College of Art (founded in 1760) merged with the university's Schools of Arts, Culture and the Environment to create an enlarged Edinburgh College of Art within the university.

In 2012/2013, 19,125 undergraduates were enrolled in the University of Edinburgh (including the Edinburgh College of Art), as were 8,565 postgraduates.

16.2 Heriot-Watt University

The university was founded in 1821 as the Edinburgh School of Arts, to provide working men with a practical knowledge of science and technology. It became associated with the inventor James Watt in 1824 to help with fundraising. In 1852, the name was altered to the Watt Institution and School of Arts, to mark the purchase of previously leased accommodation in Adam Square with funds raised in Watt's name.

The institution then broadened its focus to attract middle-class students, and in addition, was ahead of its time in accepting female students from 1869. The following year, Adam Square was demolished and the institution moved to the newly-built Chambers Street, which replaced Adam Square and two neighbouring squares. As the move had left the institution in a poor condition financially, it approached George Heriot's Trust for help. As a result of the trust's assistance, in 1885, the institution became a technical college, known as the Heriot-Watt College. In 1927, the college became independent of George Heriot's Trust.

In 1966, the college, which had already been awarding university-level degrees, became Heriot-Watt University. A move to a suburban campus at Riccarton, near Currie, began in 1969 and was completed in 1992.

Heriot-Watt merged with the Scottish College of Textiles in Galashiels (in the Scottish Borders) in 1998, creating the university's School of Textiles and Design. The university also has satellite campuses in Dubai, Malaysia and Orkney, and an associate campus in London (West London College in Mayfair).

In 2012/2013, 6,830 undergraduates were enrolled in Heriot-Watt University, as were 4,235 postgraduates.

16.3 Edinburgh Napier University

Founded in 1964 as Napier Technical College, the institution was renamed Napier College of Science and Technology two years later. In 1974, the college merged with Edinburgh College of Commerce to become Napier College of Commerce and Technology.

In 1986, the college was renamed Napier Polytechnic, and in 1992, became Napier University. Through a merger with the Scottish Borders

College of Nursing and Lothian College of Health Studies, the university acquired a Faculty of Health Studies, and in 2009, it was renamed Edinburgh Napier University.

The university has campuses at Craighouse, Craiglockhart, Merchiston and Sighthill, with smaller medical campuses at Melrose (in the Scottish Borders) and Livingstone (in West Lothian). The Merchiston campus is built around the refurbished shell of Merchiston Castle, once the home of John Napier (the inventor of logarithms), after whom the university is named.

In 2012/2013, 10,720 undergraduates were enrolled in Edinburgh Napier University, as were 2,130 postgraduates.

16.4 Queen Margaret University

Founded in 1875 as the Edinburgh School of Cookery and Domestic Economy for women only, the school originally gave lectures in what is now the National Museum of Scotland. In 1877, it moved to Shandwick Place, and in 1891, to Atholl Crescent.

The school came under the Scottish Education Department in 1909, and in 1930 it was renamed the Edinburgh College of Domestic Science. In 1970, a campus was opened at Corstorphine, and two years later, the college became Queen Margaret College (QMC).

Since then the college has been joined by the:

- Edinburgh College of Speech and Drama (established in 1929, joined QMC in 1971);
- Edinburgh School of Speech Therapy (established in 1946, joined QMC in 1975);
- Royal Infirmary of Edinburgh School of Physiotherapy (established in 1940, joined QMC in 1978);
- Astley Ainslie Hospital Occupational Therapy Training Centre (established in 1937, joined QMC in 1979);
- Edinburgh Foot Clinic and School of Chiropody (established in 1924, joined QMC in 1984);
- Edinburgh School of Radiography (established in 1936, joined QMC in 1992);
- Edinburgh University Settlement School of Art Therapy (established in 1992, joined QMC in 1997).

In 1991, the college acquired the former Leith Academy secondary school building in Duke Street as an additional campus. The college used the former Gateway Theatre in Elm Row as its drama centre, but had to close the building in 2005 due to structural faults.

From 1992, the College has been allowed to award taught degrees, and in 1998, research and higher degrees. In 1999, the college became Queen Margaret University College, and in 2007, simply Queen Margaret University.

In 2007 and 2008, the university moved to a new Musselburgh campus situated just off the A1, and it is therefore just outside the City of Edinburgh. In 2012/2013, 3,430 undergraduates were enrolled in Queen Margaret University, as were 1,905 postgraduates.

16.5 Where are the records located?
Because of Data Protection concerns, none of the universities give out information on alumni (former students) who are still alive.

The University of Edinburgh has records of alumni dating back to the very first graduating class of 1587. Students did not have to formally matriculate and graduate until the nineteenth century, however, and as a result, many of them do not appear in the records. Information on those who do has been made available in several online databases, at www.archives.lib.ed.ac.uk/alumni. Unfortunately, most of the database records contain very few details. In line with the Data Protection Act, full information is provided only for those students who graduated over seventy-five years ago, or those who are known to have died.

You can also view digitised pages of the first volume of Laureation and Degrees from 1587-1809, in which the Edinburgh University graduates signed their names.

In its archives, Heriot-Watt University has historical records of former students, such as merit lists and graduation programmes. For information, you can contact the university's Heritage and Information Governance team using the online enquiry form, at www1.hw.ac.uk/archive/enquiry-form.htm.

Chapter 17

THE STATISTICAL ACCOUNTS OF SCOTLAND

17.1 Sir John Sinclair and the Statistical Accounts

Scotland is fortunate in that Sir John Sinclair of Ulbster, MP for Caithness from 1780-1811, considered that it would be useful to have a survey of the whole country in the form of what he called 'statistical accounts'. Sir John managed to persuade the ministers of the 938 Church of Scotland parishes to produce these accounts for him, not without a certain amount of cajoling and even having to write a few accounts himself.

The ministers were sent 160 questions, of which 40 were about the geography and topography of the parish, 60 referred to its population, 16 focused on local agriculture and 44 requested information on general topics, such as the cost of living.

The first volume of the *Statistical Accounts of Scotland* was published in 1791, with a further twenty volumes having been issued by 1799. In his introduction to the first volume, Sir John said that his original intention had been simply to compile a general statistical report about Scotland, with no descriptions of individual parishes. However, he noted, 'I found such merit and ability, and so many useful facts and important observations in the answers that were sent to me, that I could not think of depriving the clergy of the credit.'

These accounts are not financial accounts, rather they are reports about the parishes, describing the landscape, crops, and types of fish in the rivers and the sea. They also discuss the price of food and clothing, how many people lived in the parish, the superstitions they adhered to and what languages they spoke, i.e. Gaelic or broad Scots.

The 'Old' *Statistical Account* published in the 1790s was very well received, so much so that a *New Statistical Account* was issued between

1834 and 1845. This time, the ministers had assistance in the form of contributions from local doctors, teachers and landowners.

A century later, a *Third Statistical Account* was produced, with a 1,044-page volume for Edinburgh published in 1966, and a smaller one for the rest of Midlothian in 1985. East Lothian even has a *Fourth Statistical Account*, which was published between 2003 and 2009.

Not many individual people are mentioned by name in the accounts. Generally, they would only be named if they were major land-owners (the 'heritors').

Sir John did try to interest England in the idea of statistical accounts, but there were few takers (such as Preston, Lancashire and St Just in Penwith, Cornwall). A *Statistical Account of Ireland* did get off the ground, but only three volumes were ever published, covering just 79 out of Ireland's nearly 1,200 parishes.

17.2 The Statistical Accounts online

You can view all of the Old and New *Statistical Accounts* free of charge online at http://edina.ac.uk/stat-acc-scot. A paid subscription (for two, six or twelve months) will give you a transcript of the text, from which you can then cut and paste to other documents. The website also provides access to some other resources, including Sir John Sinclair's analysis of the Old Accounts (published in 1826) and maps of the counties (from the New Account) showing their parishes.

There arc additional digitised copies of some of the Old and New Accounts available online at the Internet Archive, www.archive.org, and also through Google Books, http://books.google.co.uk.

You can order published volumes of the *Third Statistical Account* from online booksellers.

17.3 The Statistical Accounts for the Edinburgh area

The volumes of the *Old Statistical Account* (1791-1799) have separate entries for the parishes of Colinton, Corstorphine, Cramond, Currie, Duddingston, Edinburgh (including Canongate, St Cuthbert's, North Leith and South Leith), Kirkliston, Liberton, and Ratho – all in the county of Midlothian (or Edinburghshire) – and Dalmeny and Queensferry – then in West Lothian (or Linlithgowshire). The *New Statistical Account* (1834-1845) is similar, although Leith (North and South together) now has an entry of its own.

High Street, late nineteenth century. From Edinburgh and its Environs *(Valentine & Sons, c.1901).*

Edinburgh has a separate volume in the *Third Statistical Account*, which was published in 1966. This covers all the above parishes, except Ratho (included in the volume for Midlothian, published in 1985), Dalmeny, Kirkliston, Queensferry (all included in the West Lothian volume, published in 1992) and Currie. An account for Currie was written, but unfortunately went missing after it was returned for correction, and so it was never published.

PART THREE – APPENDICES

Appendix 1

WEBSITES FOR RESEARCHING EDINBURGH FAMILY HISTORY

A1.1 ScotlandsPeople

ScotlandsPeople, www.scotlandspeople.gov.uk, is the Scottish Government's pay-per-view family history website, providing access to images of the civil registration (statutory records of births, marriages and deaths from 1855), census returns from 1841-1911, parish registers (baptisms, marriages and burials from the sixteenth century up to 1854), Roman Catholic registers from 1703-1992, wills from 1513-1925, soldiers' wills, late nineteenth and early twentieth century valuation rolls, and coats of arms from 1672-1913.

The site uses credits, of which you can buy thirty for £7 once you've registered. You can search the indexes free of charge but (for civil registration, census, parish, Catholic and valuation records) it will cost you one credit to view a page of up to twenty-five results, and five credits (or two for valuation records) to view an image. If there is an RCE entry for a record, then this is flagged up and you can view the entry for two credits. The credits are valid for a year and any you haven't used by the time they are due to expire will be added on to any credits that you buy in the future.

Searching the indexes of wills, soldiers' wills and coats of arms is free of charge, and it will cost you ten credits to view a will, however long it is – and some are very long – ten credits to view a soldier's will, and £10 to view a coat of arms record (the earlier records don't include an illustration of the coat of arms).

For statutory births that took place less than 100 years ago, marriages

The Little family, c.1877. (Author's collection)

less than 75 years ago and deaths less than 50 years ago, you can order a certificate online (for delivery by post), which currently costs £12.

A1.2 ScotlandsPlaces

ScotlandsPlaces, www.scotlandsplaces.gov.uk, is a subscription-based Scottish Government website (although some facilities are free of charge), which has images of seventeenth and eighteenth century taxation records and nineteenth century Ordnance Survey name books. The cost of a subscription to the site is £18 for three months, £36 for six months and £72 for a year.

A1.3 National Records of Scotland

The free website of the National Records of Scotland (NRS), www.nrscotland.gov.uk, includes guides to many of the various types of records the NRS holds, a searchable index of the NRS catalogue (plus the Scottish Archive Network's catalogue of fifty-two local archives – including several Edinburgh-based archives – and the catalogue of the National Register of Archives for Scotland, which lists private papers, both in private hands and those deposited in libraries and museums).

A1.4 National Archives (London)

The website of the National Archives (TNA), www.nationalarchives. gov.uk, in Kew, London, contains pay-per-view digitised images of records of the British Army, Royal Navy, Royal Air Force and Royal Marines, including those of Scots who served in them. The site also includes guides to records on the armed forces, as well as TNA's searchable Discovery catalogue.

A1.5 National Library of Scotland

The website of the National Library of Scotland (NLS), www.nls.uk, provides free online access to digitised county maps of Scotland (many showing parish boundaries), as well as detailed town plans. The website has about seventy plans of central Edinburgh, plus nearly fifty more maps of suburban areas, including proposals for an eastward extension of the New Town between Leith Walk and Easter Road.

The NLS site also provides access to digitised versions of Post Office and other directories (see Chapter 8) and to forty open-access resources among the Library's licensed digital collections.

Victorian ladies, c.1890. (Author's collection)

Members of the Library who live in Scotland (see A2.2 below) have access to many more of these resources, such as the Bibliography of British and Irish History, Edinburgh University Press Journals Collection, Infotrac Custom Newspapers, the Dictionary of National Biography, the Oxford English Dictionary, the Scotsman Digital Archive and the Times Digital Archive.

Also hosted on the website are more than sixty features in the NLS digital gallery, which are open to everyone. These include First World War rolls of honour, over 1,800 'broadsides' (news-sheets, often scandalous), 300 early photographs, genealogies of some ancient Scottish families, gazetteers of Scotland, more than 70 seventeenth-century engravings, biographies of eminent Scots, and 137 photographs of the south side of Edinburgh.

A1.6 Ancestry.co.uk

The subscription-based website Ancestry.co.uk, www.ancestry.co.uk, includes British Army service records (including those for Scots) from the time of the First World War, as well as digitised copies of a few issues of some eighteenth and nineteenth century Edinburgh newspapers.

A1.7 Findmypast.co.uk

The subscription-based website Findmypast.co.uk, www.findmypast. co.uk, also includes British Army service records from the time of the First World War, as well as those from 1760-1915. The site also holds records of the East India Company (including British Indian baptisms, marriages, burials and wills), as well as a large collection of British newspapers (including the *Caledonian Mercury* from 1720-1867; the *Edinburgh Evening Courant* from 1828-1869; and the *Edinburgh Evening News* from 1873-1942).

A1.8 Deceased Online

Deceased Online, www.deceasedonline.com, is a pay-per-view and subscription-based website, with digitised images of burial and cremation records from a number of cemeteries and crematoria, including some of those in Edinburgh (see Chapter 10).

A1.9 Capital Collections

The Capital Collections website, www.capitalcollections.org.uk, has many images of Edinburgh, taken from the collections of its museums, libraries and galleries. You can browse the images by place or by topic. The site also has a number of online exhibitions.

A1.10 Our Town Stories

The Our Town Stories website, www.ourtownstories.co.uk, displays a map of Edinburgh with 'pins' on it. Clicking on a blue pin brings up a story about Edinburgh, on a yellow pin a historic map, and on an orange pin an image. Many of the latter are 'then and now' images, in which an old photograph is superimposed on a current one. Moving a slider control to the left allows you to see only the old photo, and to the right only the new one, while moving it to a central position lets you see both.

A1.11 Newhaven-on-Forth

The Newhaven Action Trust (also known as Newhaven Heritage) has set up the Newhaven-on-Forth website, www.newhavenonforth. org.uk, to celebrate Newhaven's people and its history. The group plan to set up a heritage centre in Newhaven with a museum, café, shop, meeting rooms, genealogy centre and educational facilities.

A1.12 My Ain Folk

Kirsty F. Wilkinson's website, www.myainfolk.com, includes a free 24-page list of pre-1841 Scottish population listings, including a number for the Edinburgh area. The site also has a free 44-page list of records of the Scottish poor, including those for Edinburgh and Leith.

Appendix 2

EDINBURGH ARCHIVES

A2.1 National Records of Scotland (and ScotlandsPeople Centre)
General Register House, 2 Princes Street, Edinburgh EH1 3YY.
Tel: 0131 535 1314 (switchboard); 0131 314 4411 (to order birth, marriage or death certificates); 0131 314 4300 (ScotlandsPeople Centre, to book seats, etc.)
Website: www.nrscotland.gov.uk
Email: Use the Feedback/Contact Form on the website.

The National Records of Scotland (NRS) was created in 2011 by the merger of the General Register Office for Scotland and the National Archives of Scotland (which had previously been known as the Scottish Record Office).

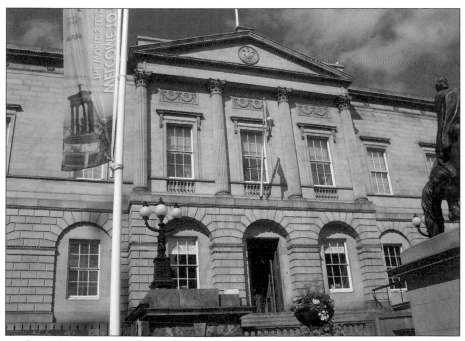

General Register House, 2014. (Author's collection)

The NRS holds records relating to a large number of topics, including churches, craftsmen (for the Edinburgh area: carters, goldsmiths, shoemakers, tailors, wrights and masons), crime, inheritance, land, military records pre-1707, mining, poor relief, railways and taxation.

The ScotlandsPeople Centre is situated in General Register House and the neighbouring New Register House. There you can view all the records available online at the ScotlandsPeople website, plus birth, marriage and death records up to the present day.

A day search pass for the ScotlandsPeople Centre costs £15, while searching in the NRS Historical Search Room is free of charge. The ScotlandsPeople Centre part of the NRS website has a large list of 'Useful Websites for Family History Research'.

A2.2 National Library of Scotland

George IV Bridge, Edinburgh, EH1 1EW.
Tel: 0131 623 3700
Website: www.nls.uk
Email: enquiries@nls.uk (to pre-order material for the General Reading Room), otherwise use the 'Ask a Librarian' query form on the website.

The National Library of Scotland (NLS) describes itself as 'the world's leading centre for the study of Scotland and the Scots'. At its main building in George IV Bridge, the Library has a General Reading Room for journals, newspapers and printed books, as well as a Special Collections Reading Room for manuscripts, music and rare books, and a Multimedia Reading Room. At another NLS building in Causewayside, there is a Maps Reading Room for maps, atlases and gazetteers.

Anyone can obtain a library card free of charge to use the NLS collections, and if you live in Scotland, you can have online access to 147 of the NLS's licensed digital collections (if you live elsewhere, then your access is limited to forty of the collections). There are also a further nineteen licensed digital collections that you can use only in the Library.

A2.3 Edinburgh City Archives

Level 1, City Chambers, 253 High Street, Edinburgh, EH1 1YJ
Tel: 0131 529 4616

Website: www.edinburgh.gov.uk/info/20032/access_to_information
/600/edinburgh_city_archives
Email: archives@edinburgh.gov.uk

Edinburgh City Archives (ECA) holds the official historical records for
Edinburgh City Council and its predecessors, as well as records created
by businesses, clubs and societies, organisations and individuals.

You can find top-level descriptions of the records held by the ECA
('GB236') in the online catalogue of the Scottish Archive Network
(SCAN), at www.scan.org.uk/catalogue. From the ECA website, you can
download a file describing the general, army and militia, burgess and
trade, burgh/bailie court, church, parochial board and poorhouse, police,
and school board records held by the archives. The site also has two lists
of collections with ECA reference numbers and covering dates.

In addition, you can download: an index of Edinburgh Poll Tax
returns for 1694-1699 for all parishes of the city as it was then; a register
of aliens covering the years 1798-1825; the paupers' claims book of the
St Cuthbert's Parochial Board for 1850-1852; and a register of the
inmates of Edinburgh Charity Workhouse from 1 July 1835 to 30 June
1841 (with some later death dates).

A2.4 Edinburgh Central Library

George IV Bridge, Edinburgh, EH1 1EG
Tel: 0131 242 8070
Website: www.edinburgh.gov.uk/info/20012/libraries/183/trace_your
_family_tree
Email: central.edinburghandscottish.library@edinburgh.gov.uk

The Edinburgh and Scottish Collection at Edinburgh Central Library
contains: Church of Scotland parish records from 1600-1854; census
returns from 1841-1901; electoral registers from 1832 to the present;
valuation rolls for Edinburgh from 1914 to the present (for Midlothian
from 1907-2001 and for West Lothian from 1922-2001); the indexes of
services of heirs from 1700-1969; and the index of sasines.

The collection also holds trade and Post Office directories from 1752-
1974, telephone directories from 1940 to the present date, newspapers
(including *The Scotsman* from 1817 onwards and the *Edinburgh Evening
News* from 1873), monumental inscriptions, burial records, and

publications of the Scottish Record Society (including lists of burgesses, guild rolls, and apprentice records).

You'll also find maps and images (drawings, paintings, photographs, engravings and postcards) in the collection. Many of the images are available online at the Capital Collections website (see A1.9 above).

Appendix 3

EDINBURGH FAMILY HISTORY SOCIETY

A3.1 Scottish Genealogy Society

15 Victoria Terrace, Edinburgh, EH1 2JL
Tel: 0131 220 3677
Website: www.scotsgenealogy.com
Email: enquiries@scotsgenealogy.com

Founded in 1953, the Scottish Genealogy Society is Scotland's oldest genealogical organisation, and it has built up a library of more than 4,000 books and CDs on family history and related topics.

The society runs a programme of classes in its Family History Centre at the above address. The classes cost £10 each and are held from 10.00 am to midday on Saturdays, for both members and non-members.

From its website, you can download sections of the society's 'black book', which contains details of all of its Scottish death and burial holdings. The relevant sections for the City of Edinburgh unitary authority area are the Edinburgh, Midlothian and West Lothian county lists.

The society's online shop sells various Edinburgh-related items, including nineteenth century Post Office Directories on CD; pictorial history books (Old Cramond; Old Currie, Balerno and Juniper Green; Old Leith; and South Edinburgh); a list of Trinity House Leith pilots 1797-1922; more than twenty monumental inscription collections for the Edinburgh area in book or CD format; Tron Church parish Poll Tax listing 1694; West Lothian Hearth Tax listing 1691; guides to occupations (candlemakers, clock- and watchmakers, and photographers); church records from the kirk session rolls; and burial records.

Membership of the society costs £20 a year for an individual and £25 for a family in the UK, and £25 overseas. Members receive the society's quarterly magazine *The Scottish Genealogist*, 10 per cent discount on most publications, and free access to the library and Family History Centre.

Appendix 4

EDINBURGH MUSEUMS

A4.1 National Museum of Scotland
Chambers Street, Edinburgh, EH1 1JF
Tel: 0300 123 6789
Website: www.nms.ac.uk/national-museum-of-scotland
Email: info@nms.ac.uk

The National Museum of Scotland was founded in 2006, made up of the new Museum of Scotland (opened in 1998) and its neighbour, the Royal Museum. The latter had been created in 1985 from the organisational merger of the Royal Scottish Museum (formerly known as the Industrial Museum of Scotland, partially opened in 1866, and renamed in 1904) and the National Museum of Antiquities of Scotland, which opened in 1891. The collections of the former Royal Scottish Museum and the National Museum of Antiquities of Scotland remained in separate buildings until 1995.

The newer National Museum of Scotland building is dedicated to presenting Scottish history in chronological order, while the older building (which was extensively refurbished and re-organised between 2008 and 2011) covers natural history, world cultures, European art and design, and science and technology.

The museum's exhibits range from an ancient Assyrian relief of King Ashurnasirpal, excavated near Mosul in Iraq, to the stuffed body of Dolly the Sheep, the first mammal to be created through cloning in 1996. Other items in the museum include Roman remains from Cramond, Pictish stones, the Jacobite and Hanoverian flags raised at the Battle of Culloden in 1746, a sixteenth century Scottish form of guillotine, and one of Elton John's suits.

Museum of Scotland, 2005 (Available under a Creative Commons Attribution-Share Alike 3.0 Unported licence at http://commons.wikimedia.org/wiki/File:Museum_of_Scotland.jpg)

A4.2 Museum of Edinburgh (formerly Huntly House Museum)

142 Canongate, Edinburgh, EH8 8DD
Tel: 0131 529 4143
Website: www.edinburghmuseums.org.uk/Venues/Museum-of-Edinburgh
Email: Use the contact form on the website.

The museum is housed in a series of sixteenth to eighteenth century buildings in Bakehouse Close, which had more than 300 tenants at the time of the 1851 census. Part of the museum's building was formerly known as Huntly House, in which the Dowager Duchess of Gordon was thought to have lived in the eighteenth century. The house was named after Huntly Castle in Aberdeenshire, which was the ancestral home of the chiefs of Clan Gordon.

Huntly House and the neighbouring Acheson House were bought by Edinburgh Council in the 1920s and opened in 1932 as Huntly House Museum (to house the City Museum collections, previously displayed in the City Chambers). The museum was extended in 1969, renamed the Museum of Edinburgh in 2001 and further extended in 2012.

Exhibits on display within the museum include the National Covenant of 1638, James Craig's 1766 plan for the New Town, and the collar and bowl of the Skye terrier 'Greyfriars Bobby'. In addition, the museum holds collections of cut and engraved glass, silverware, longcase clocks, and Scottish pottery and china.

A4.3 The People's Story Museum
163 Canongate, Edinburgh, EH8 8BN
Tel: 0131 529 4057
Website: www.edinburghmuseums.org.uk/Venues/The-People-s-Story
Email: Use the contact form on the website.

The museum is housed in the Canongate Tolbooth, which was built in 1591 on the site of an earlier tollbooth. This was the courthouse, prison and council chamber of the Burgh of Canongate, administered separately from Edinburgh until it was incorporated in the city in 1856. After various uses, the building became a museum in 1954.

After alterations, the museum was reopened in 1989 as The People's Story, which tells of the working and social lives of Edinburgh people from the late eighteenth century to the present day. There are collections on 'Edinburgh Life', 'Working Life in Edinburgh' and 'At Home in Edinburgh', as well as those on Leith and Newhaven.

A4.4 The Writers' Museum
Lady Stair's Close, Edinburgh, EH1 2PA
Tel: 0131 529 4901
Website: www.edinburghmuseums.org.uk/Venues/The-Writers--Museum
Email: Use the contact form on the website.

The Writers' Museum tells the stories of Robert Burns, Sir Walter Scott and Robert Louis Stevenson. The museum is located in Lady Stair's House, built in 1622 by Sir William Gray of Pittendrum, an Edinburgh merchant, and associated with the Dowager Countess of Stair, who lived there in the early eighteenth century.

The museum's collections include Burns's writing desk, Scott's rocking horse and Stevenson's riding boots and ring. In addition, the museum holds first editions of Scott's *Waverley* and Stevenson's *A Child's Garden of Verses*, as well as Burns's manuscript draft of 'Scots Wha Hae' (Bruce's address to his troops before the Battle of Bannockburn).

A4.5 Museum of Childhood
42 High Street, Edinburgh, EH1 1TG
Tel: 0131 529 4142
Website: www.edinburghmuseums.org.uk/Venues/Museum-of-Childhood
Email: Use the contact form on the website.

The museum moved to the eastern side of South Gray's Close in the High Street in 1957, having outgrown its previous home in Lady Stair's House Museum. In 1982, it expanded into the western side too, the ground and first floors of which had become a theatre around 1760. The enlarged museum opened in 1986.

The museum's collections include a reconstruction of a Victorian street with outdoor toys, early Steiff bears, an eighteenth century 'Queen Anne' doll, and a doll's house with more than 2,000 items in twenty one rooms. There is also an 1880s butcher's shop, complete with prime cuts of 'meat' and a miniature butcher.

A4.6 Queensferry Museum
53 High Street, South Queensferry, EH30 9HP
Tel: 0131 331 5545
Website: www.edinburghmuseums.org.uk/Venues/Queensferry-Museum
Email: Use the contact form on the website.

The museum is housed in the former Viewforth Temperance Hotel, which was also used as the Norwegian Naval Command (Port Edgar) between 1942 and 1944. The building then became the Royal Burgh of Queensferry's council chambers from 1945–1975, at which point Queensferry was absorbed by Edinburgh.

There are exhibits on the historic ferry service over the Firth of Forth to Fife prior to the opening of the Forth Road Bridge in 1964, the building of the Forth Rail and Road Bridges, the former Royal Naval base at Port Edgar, and many photographs of Queensferry's local customs and traditions.

A4.7 Museum on the Mound
The Mound, Edinburgh, EH1 1YZ
Tel: 0131 243 5464
Website: www.museumonthemound.com
Email: info@museumonthemound

This museum of money opened in 2006 within the former Bank of Scotland headquarters. Its displays tell of the bank's foundation in 1695, illustrate Edinburgh's growth using interactive maps, show the evolution of money over the last 4,000 years, describe the rise of building societies, let you experience life assurance in the 1820s and describe what working for a bank in the nineteenth and twentieth centuries was like.

A4.8 Surgeons' Hall Museum
Nicolson Street, Edinburgh, EH8 9DW
Tel: 0131 527 1711/1600
Website: www.museum.rcsed.ac.uk
Email: museum@rcsed.ac.uk

The museum is located in Surgeons' Hall, designed by William Henry Playfair and completed in 1832 as the home of the Royal College of Surgeons of Edinburgh. The museum has been redeveloped and was scheduled to reopen in September 2015. Among its exhibits is the death mask of William Burke, of the notorious Edinburgh body-snatchers Burke and Hare, who was hanged in 1829.

The museum's permanent exhibitions include a pathology museum, history of surgery, dental collection, 'The Real Sherlock Holmes' (about the surgeon Joseph Bell, whose deductive skills inspired Sir Arthur Conan Doyle to write his detective stories), 'Sight for Scotland: 100 Years of Ophthalmology', '60 Years of Surgery 1952-2012', and 'Skin Deep: the Restoration of Form and Function' (about the development of cosmetic surgery).

Appendix 5

EDINBURGH ART GALLERIES

A5.1 Scottish National Gallery/Royal Scottish Academy

The Mound, Edinburgh, EH2 2EL
Tel: 0131 624 6200
Website: www.nationalgalleries.org/visit/introduction-114
Email: nginfo@nationalgalleries.org

The Scottish National Gallery originated in the Royal Institution for the Encouragement of the Fine Arts in Scotland, which was founded in 1819, when it began to acquire paintings.

The Royal Scottish Academy (RSA) was founded in 1826, with the aims of holding an annual exhibition, opening an Academy of Fine Arts to teach students free of charge, establishing a library, providing charitable funds for less well-off artists, and admitting eminent artists as honorary members.

A building designed by William Henry Playfair was erected for the Royal Institution on the Mound, near Princes Street, and was opened in 1828. The building was shared with the RSA from 1835. Playfair designed a second building, situated behind the first, for a National Gallery of Scotland, for which Prince Albert laid the foundation stone in 1850. The RSA shared this building, and held its first exhibition there in 1855.

Following a Government report in 1903, the RSA took over the former Royal Institution building in 1910, at the same time gifting 96 paintings and sculptures and around 2,000 drawings to the National Gallery of Scotland.

Basement galleries were added to the National Gallery in 1970, and in the early years of the twenty-first century, the two buildings were linked by a newly constructed underground area. Now known as the Gardens Entrance, this was opened in 2004 to provide access from East Princes Street Gardens.

Edinburgh Castle and National Gallery of Scotland, late nineteenth century. From Edinburgh and its Environs *(Valentine & Sons, c.1901).*

The Scottish National Gallery (as the combined buidings are now called), holds many paintings by Scottish artists, such as David Allan, William Dyce, Andrew Geddes, James Guthrie, Gavin Hamilton, Robert Scott Lauder, Horatio McCulloch, William York Macgregor, William MacTaggart, John Phillip, Sir Henry Raeburn, Allan Ramsay, David Roberts, William Strang and Sir David Wilkie. In addition, there are works in the gallery by the internationally renowned artists Botticelli, Cézanne, Constable, Degas, Delacroix, Dürer, van Dyck, Gainsborough, Gauguin, van Gogh, Goya, El Greco, Holbein, Ingres, Leonardo da Vinci, Monet, Pissarro, Poussin, Raphael, Rembrandt, Sir Joshua

Reynolds, Rubens, Seurat, Tintoretto, Titian, Turner, Velázquez, Vermeer, Watteau and many others.

The RSA building is used to host exhibitions, and contains the academy's offices.

A5.2 Scottish National Gallery of Modern Art
75 Belford Road, Edinburgh, EH4 3DR
Tel: 0131 624 6200
Website: www.nationalgalleries.org/visit/introduction-118
Email: gmainfo@nationalgalleries.org

When the gallery was opened in 1960, its original home was in Inverleith House within the Royal Botanic Garden of Edinburgh. In 1980, the gallery moved to its present location in the former John Watson's Institution (see Chapter 15).

The gallery's collections include sculptures by Henry Moore, Barbara Hepworth and Eduardo Paolozzi, and paintings by Francis Bacon, Lucian Freud, Roy Lichtenstein, Matisse, Mondrian, Ben Nicholson, Picasso, Andy Warhol and the Scottish Colourists (Francis Cadell, John Duncan Fergusson, Leslie Hunter and Samuel Peploe).

A5.3 Scottish National Portrait Gallery
1 Queen Street, Edinburgh, EH2 1JD
Tel: 0131 624 6200
Website: www.nationalgalleries.org/visit/introduction-298
Email: pginfo@nationalgalleries.org

In the late eighteenth century, David Erskine, 11th Earl of Buchan, collected a number of Scottish portraits, many of which are now in the gallery. There was interest in Scotland in the nineteenth century in establishing a portrait gallery along the same lines as the National Portrait Gallery in London.

Accordingly, a Scottish National Portrait Gallery was founded in 1882, and to house its collections a new building was completed in 1889, the cost of which was met by John Ritchie Findlay, proprietor of *The Scotsman* newspaper. Until 2009, the gallery's building was shared with the National Museum of Antiquities (now part of the National Museum of Scotland – see Appendix 4.1).

The gallery holds around 3,000 paintings and sculptures, 25,000 prints and drawings, and 38,000 photographs. The subjects of the portraits range from historical figures such as Mary, Queen of Scots (painted posthumously), James VI, Charles I, Robert Burns, Sir Walter Scott, and 'Bonnie Prince Charlie', to celebrated present-day Scots, including Sir Alex Ferguson, Billy Connolly and Robbie Coltrane.

A5.4 City Art Centre
2 Market Street, Edinburgh, EH1 1DE
Tel: 0131 529 3993
Website: www.edinburghmuseums.org.uk/Venues/City-Art-Centre
Email: Use contact form on website.

The City Art Centre was founded in 1980 in a nine-storey former warehouse built between 1899 and 1902 for *The Scotsman* newspaper. With galleries on six floors, the centre has a collection of around 4,500 works of art dating from the seventeenth century to the present day.

Many of the centre's paintings depict Edinburgh, including 'The Entry of George IV into Edinburgh, 1822' by John Wilson Ewbank, 'The Port of Leith, 1824' by Alexander Nasmyth, 'Horse Fair in the Grassmarket' (c.1830) by James Howe, and 'Great Junction Street' (1998) by Jock McFadyen.

Appendix 6

PALACE AND CASTLES OF EDINBURGH

A6.1 Holyrood Palace and ruins of Holyrood Abbey
Canongate, Edinburgh, EH8 8DX
Tel: 0131 556 5100 (bookings)
Website: www.royalcollection.org.uk/visit/palace-of-holyroodhouse
Email: bookinginfo@royalcollection.org.uk

The palace that stands at the foot of the Canongate, near the recently-built Scottish Parliament building, originated in Holyrood Abbey. King David I, who had spent many years at the court of his brother-in-law, Henry I of England, founded the abbey in 1128 and brought there a community of Augustinian canons from Merton in Surrey. About sixty years later, the simple church in which the canons had worshipped was replaced by a much larger building.

The abbey's position, relatively near the border with England, and its royal connections made it a target for English attacks. In 1322 and 1385, the abbey was particularly badly damaged, as it was once again in 1544, when it was burned and sacked by the Earl of Hertford's army during Henry VIII's 'Rough Wooing' of Mary, Qeen of Scots. The abbey was attacked yet again in 1547. By the medieval period, it had become an important royal residence, and in 1430, James I chose Holyrood as the birthplace of his son, crowned James II in 1437, on the assassination of his father in Perth.

From 1501-1505, James IV greatly extended the abbey's living quarters with the first stages in the construction of Holyrood Palace for himself and his queen, Margaret Tudor, daughter of Henry VII of England. James V added a tower between 1529 and 1532 for himself and his future second queen, Mary of Guise (also known as Mary of Lorraine).

The daughter of James and Mary, succeeded her father as Mary, Queen of Scots, just a few days after her birth in December 1542. When Mary returned to Scotland in August 1561, after the death of her first husband King François II of France, she lived at Holyrood for much of the time.

In July 1565, Mary married Henry Stuart, Lord Darnley, in the chapel at Holyrood. Almost a year later, King Henry (as Darnley had become by then) was the principal conspirator in the murder of his wife's Italian secretary, David Rizzio. Henry was himself murdered in February 1567, after which Mary married James Hepburn, Earl of Bothwell, in May of the same year, again at Holyrood.

The son of Henry and Mary, James VI, spent much time at Holyrood, when his queen consort, Anne of Denmark, was crowned in 1590. In 1603, however, James succeeded to the throne of England as James I (through his great-grandmother, Margaret Tudor), and moved to England, after which Holyrood lost its importance.

The palace was rebuilt in the 1670s for Charles II, although he never saw the results of the work. The king's brother James, Duke of Albany and York, and his second wife, Mary of Modena, lived at Holyrood at

Holyrood Palace, 1745. From Francis H Groome, Ordnance Gazetteer of Scotland *(Thomas C Jack, 1885).*

Arthur's Seat and Holyrood Palace, late nineteenth century. From Edinburgh and its Environs *(Valentine & Sons, c.1901).*

various times between 1679 and 1682. After James succeeded his brother as James VII (and II of England), he ordered in 1687 the expulsion from the chapel of the parishioners of Canongate, who used the surviving nave of the abbey as their parish church. The nave was then converted into a Chapel Royal for Roman Catholic worship. At the end of the following year, however, the chapel was ransacked by a mob during the 'Glorious Revolution', which saw James's deposition from the English and Scottish thrones.

The palace's Great Gallery contains 89 of the 110 portraits of the Kings of Scots (from the legendary sixth-century Fergus Mór mac Eirc to James VII), painted by the Dutch artist Jacob de Wet from 1684-1686. The Scottish genealogist Sir Iain Moncreiffe called them 'every Scotsman's family portrait gallery'. While allowing that 'the Stewart portraits may be tolerable likenesses', Sir Iain felt it was 'likely that ordinary folk from the Canongate posed for the more ancient kings.'

During the 1745 Jacobite rebellion, Prince Charles Edward Stuart ('Bonnie Prince Charlie') stayed at Holyrood and held court there briefly. In 1758, an attempt was made to avoid the collapse of the abbey church by vaulting the roof in stone, but the work was done badly and the roof collapsed in a storm ten years later, leaving the church a ruin.

The members of the French royal family who had survived the 1789 revolution lived at Holyrood for a time, including the Comte d'Artois (younger brother of the executed King Louis XVI), who succeeded to the French throne as Charles X in 1824. Once more exiled in 1831, Charles returned to Holyrood.

In 1822, George IV became the first British monarch to travel to Scotland since Charles I. Following the King's visit to Holyrood, the palace was brought back into a state of good repair, although plans to restore the nave within the abbey church were not proceeded with

A century later, King George V and Queen Mary made Holyrood a family home, continuing the work carried out in the 1670s. Since then, Holyrood Palace has become a regular royal residence.

A6.2 Edinburgh Castle
Castle Hill, Edinburgh, EH1 2NG
Tel: 0131 225 9846
Website: www.edinburghcastle.gov.uk
Email: ec.enquiries@scotland.gsi.gov.uk

The castle stands on a lava plug from Edinburgh's 350,000,000-year-old extinct volcano. On the castle rock, traces of late Bronze Age roundhouses have been found which date back to c.900 BC, as well as Roman remains from nearly 2,000 years ago.

The oldest surviving building in the castle is St Margaret's Chapel, probably built by King David I as a memorial to his mother, Queen Margaret (the wife of King Malcolm III, 'Malcolm Canmore'), who was canonised in 1250.

The early castle was dismantled by order of King Robert I, 'Robert the Bruce', after it had been recaptured from the English in 1314, shortly before the Battle of Bannockburn. The later castle included the royal palace that was the birthplace in 1566 of the future King James VI (who became King James I of England in 1603), son of Mary, Queen of Scots and her husband King Henry (Lord Darnley).

Today's castle includes the royal palace, the Scottish National War Memorial (see Chapter 10), the 'Honours of Scotland' (the sceptre presented to King James IV by Pope Alexander VI around 1494, the sword presented to the same king by Pole Julius II in 1507, and the crown made for King James V in 1540), and the 'Stone of Destiny'

Edinburgh Castle, 1715. From Francis H Groome, Ordnance Gazetteer of Scotland *(Thomas C Jack, 1885).*

(removed from Scone Abbey in 1296 by King Edward I of England, and returned to Scotland by the United Kingdom Prime Minister John Major in 1996), and the regimental museums of the Royal Scots and the Royal Scots Dragoon Guards.

Also in the castle is 'Mons Meg', a giant siege gun made at Mons, now in Belgium, in 1449 and presented to King James II in 1457 by Philip the Good, Duke of Burgundy, James's uncle-by-marriage.

Every day since June 1861 (except Sundays, Good Friday and Christmas Day – and for periods during the First and Second World Wars), a gun is fired on Mills Mount Battery at 1.00 pm, known as 'the one o'clock gun'.

A6.3 Lauriston Castle
2a Cramond Road South, Davidson's Mains, Edinburgh, EH4 5QD
Tel: 0131 336 2060
Website: www.edinburghmuseums.org.uk/Venues/Lauriston-Castle
Email: Use the contact form on the website.

Lauriston Castle was built about 1593 as a tower house by Sir Archibald Napier for his younger son Alexander, half-brother of John Napier, the inventor of logarithms.

An extension was added between 1824 and 1827 for Thomas Allen, an Edinburgh banker who owned the *Caledonian Mercury* newspaper. In 1870, a library was added in a new upper storey in the servants' wing.

The gardens were laid out in the 1840s by William Henry Playfair, and a Japanese garden (the Edinburgh-Kyoto Friendship Garden) opened in 2002.

The last private owners, the Reids, who had no children, left their beautifully decorated house to the city of Edinburgh, with the proviso that it should not be altered. The castle is now run by the City of Edinburgh Council's Museums and Galleries department.

A6.4 Ruins of Craigmillar Castle
Craigmillar Castle Road, Edinburgh, EH16 4SY
Tel: 0131 661 4445
Website: www.historic-scotland.gov.uk (search for 'Craigmillar Castle overview')
Email: Use the feedback form on the Historic Scotland website.

Craigmillar Castle was built in the late fourteenth century for the Preston family, who were for over 300 years feudal barons of Craigmillar, in the parish of Liberton. The castle was extended in the fifteenth and sixteenth centuries, and in 1660, it was bought by Sir John Gilmour, Lord President of the Court of Session.

In the eighteenth century, the Gilmour family left the castle, and by 1775, it had fallen into a ruined state. The property is now looked after by Historic Scotland, which describes it as 'one of Scotland's most perfectly preserved castles'.

King James V lived at the castle for a time in the sixteenth century to avoid an outbreak of the plague. His daughter Mary, Queen of Scots spent a little over two weeks at the castle towards the end of 1566, after she had given birth to the future James VI at Edinburgh Castle. At Craigmillar Castle, Queen Mary is alleged to have plotted the murder of her husband King Henry (Lord Darnley).

In 1842, it was proposed to restore the castle for Queen Victoria's use, but this did not take place, although the queen did visit the castle in 1886.

BIBLIOGRAPHY

History
James E Fraser, *The Roman Conquest of Scotland* (The History Press, 2005)

Michael Fry, *Edinburgh* (Macmillan, 2009)

Geoff Holder, *Bloody Scottish History: Edinburgh* (The History Press, 2012)

George Scott-Moncrieff, *Edinburgh* (B.T. Batsford, 1947)

Sacheverell Sitwell and Francis Bamford, *Edinburgh* (Faber and Faber, 1938)

Edward Topham, *Edinburgh Life 100 Years Ago* selected and arranged from 'Captain Topham's Letters' [written in 1774 and 1775] (William Brown, 1886) *

Topography
Malcolm Cant, *Villages of Edinburgh, Volumes 1 and 2* (John Donald, 1986 and 1987)

Richard Fawcett, *The Palace of Holyroodhouse* (Her Majesty's Stationery Office, 1988)

Francis H Groome ed., *Ordnance Gazetteer of Scotland: A Survey of Scottish Topography, Statistical, Biographical and Historical* (Thomas C. Jack, 1885) *

Stuart Harris, *The Place Names of Edinburgh* (Gordon Wright, 1996)

Theo Lang ed., *The Queen's Scotland: Edinburgh and the Lothians* (Hodder and Stoughton, 1952)

Colin McWilliam, *Edinburgh New Town Guide* (Edinburgh New Town Conservation Committee, 2nd edition, 1984)

Chris Tabraham ed., *Edinburgh Castle* (Historic Scotland, 1994)

W J Watson, *The Celtic Place Names of Scotland* (Birlinn, 2004)

The *Statistical Accounts* of Scotland
Sir John Sinclair, Bart. ed., *The Statistical Account of Scotland, Volume 6* (William Creech, 1793) *

Society for the Benefit of the Sons and Daughters of the Clergy ed., *The New Statistical Account of Scotland, Volume 1: [County of] Edinburgh* (William Blackwood and Sons, 1845) *
David Keir ed., *The Third Statistical Account of Scotland: The City of Edinburgh* (Collins, 1966)
Hilary Kirkland ed., *The Third Statistical Account of Scotland: The County of Midlothian* (Scottish Academic Press, 1985)

Literature
Andrew Lownie, *The Edinburgh Literary Companion* (Polygon, 2005)

Scottish Family History
Rosemary Bigwood, *The Scottish Family Tree Detective* (Manchester University Press, 2006)
Tristram Clarke, *Tracing Your Scottish Ancestors* (Birlinn, revised 6th edition, 2012)
Bruce Durie, *Scottish Genealogy* (The History Press, 3rd edition, 2012)
Gerald Hamilton-Edwards, *In Search of Scottish Ancestry* (Phillimore, 2nd edition, 1983)
Sherry Irvine, *Scottish Ancestry* (Ancestry, revised edition, 2003)
Linda Jonas and Paul Milner, *Discovering Your Scottish Ancestors* (Betterway Books, 2002)
Ian Maxwell, *Tracing Your Scottish Ancestors* (Pen and Sword, 2nd edition, 2013)
Chris Paton, *Researching Scottish Family History* (Family History Partnership, 2010)
D J Steel, *Sources for Scottish Genealogy and Family History* (Society of Genealogists, 1970)
Alan Stewart, *Gathering the Clans: Tracing Scottish Ancestry on the Internet* (Phillimore, 2004)
Alan Stewart, *My Ancestor was Scottish* (Society of Genealogists, 2012)

General
James Bone, *The Perambulator in Edinburgh* (Jonathan Cape, 1926)
Robert Chambers, *Traditions of Edinburgh* (W&R Chambers, 1868) *
David Daiches ed., *Edinburgh: A Traveller's Companion* (Constable, 1986)
Geological Museum, *Volcanoes* (Her Majesty's Stationery Office, 1974)

J Gilhooley, *A Directory of Edinburgh in 1752* (Edinburgh University Press, 1988)

D L G Hunter, *Edinburgh's Transport* (The Advertiser Press, 1964)

John and Julia Keay, *Collins Encyclopaedia of Scotland* (HarperCollins, 1994)

Ralph Lownie ed., *Auld Reekie: An Edinburgh Anthology* (Mainstream Publishing, 2004)

David McAdam, *Edinburgh and West Lothian: A Landscape Fashioned by Geology* (Scottish Natural Heritage, 2003) – available to download as a PDF file free of charge at www.snh.gov.uk

Moray McLaren, *The Capital of Scotland* (Douglas and Foulis, 1950)

Michael Turnbull, *Edinburgh Portraits* (John Donald, 1987)

David Stewart Valentine, *Leith at Random* (Porthole, 2005)

Francis Watt, *The Book of Edinburgh Anecdote* (T N Foulis, 1912) *

Christopher Winn, *I Never Knew That About Scotland* (Ebury Press, 2007)

Gordon Wright, Ian Adams and Michael Scott, *A Guide to Holyrood Park and Arthur's Seat* (Gordon Wright, 1987)

(*Available to download as a PDF file free of charge at https:// archive.org.)

INDEX